THE HOPEFUL FAMILY

*Raising Resilient
Children in
Uncertain Times*

Amelia Richardson Dress

Morehouse Publishing
NEW YORK

Unless otherwise noted, the Scripture quotations contained herein are from the New Revised Standard Version Bible, copyright © 1989 by the Division of Christian Education of the National Council of Churches of Christ in the U.S.A. Used by permission. All rights reserved.

Morehouse Publishing, 19 East 34th Street, New York, NY 10016

Morehouse Publishing is an imprint of Church Publishing Incorporated. www.churchpublishing.org

Cover art and design by Gillian Whiting
Interior design and typesetting by Beth Oberholtzer

Names and details have been changed for privacy. Stories have sometimes been condensed for clarity.

Parts of this book were drawn from previous writing I did for Spiritual Parent, spiritualparent.org, or my personal blog, barefootfamily.me.

Library of Congress Cataloging-in-Publication Data

Names: Richardson Dress, Amelia, author.
Title: The hopeful family : raising resilient children in uncertain times / Amelia Richardson Dress.
Identifiers: LCCN 2020035646 (print) | LCCN 2020035647 (ebook) | ISBN 9781640653849 (paperback) | ISBN 9781640653856 (epub)
Subjects: LCSH: Parenting–Religious aspects–Christianity. | Child rearing–Religious aspects–Christianity. | Christian education–Home training. | Christian education of children.
Classification: LCC BV4529 .R534 2021 (print) | LCC BV4529 (ebook) | DDC
248.8/45–dc23
LC record available at https://lccn.loc.gov/2020035646
LC ebook record available at https://lccn.loc.gov/2020035647

For Isabel, who encouraged me when I needed it most. You are wise beyond your years.

And for Abe, who celebrated every milestone. Huzzah!

Contents

Acknowledgments

With gratitude:

In the past ten years, I've been thrilled to discover that the writing world is full of encouragers. From Donna Rafanello, who went above and beyond to coach me through my very first article, to the editors and authors who reviewed and encouraged this book along the way, I am so grateful. Every time I try to list you all, I run out of space. But I know who you are and I am better for knowing you.

Wendy Claire Barrie, Ryan Masteller, and the entire team at CPI who took this book from manuscript to a thoughtfully laid-out book, thank you. I was consistently impressed with your care and touched by your encouragement. Wendy, your questions and prompts always helped me think deeply. It was a rich experience to work with you.

My colleagues at Garfield County Department of Human Services were among the first people to explore the connections between spirituality and resilience with me. Thank you, Donna, Dana, and Ericka. I wish every young mother had mentors like you.

My ideals of what church can be are forever tied to a memory of talking theology with the Ladies Guild in the basement of New Castle Congregational Church. Thank you for welcoming an earnest teenager into your midst. And for the churches I've been part of since then, thank you for living up to the high bar that was set for you. I am especially grateful for the colleagues and parishioners who reminded me to make time for my writing. May each of you also pursue the things that bring you happiness.

It's not an exaggeration to say that I have the best friends, neighbors, and colleagues. I hope that shines through in the stories I shared here.

I count it as a blessing to have grown up with the guidance of parents like Katherine and Lynn Richardson, and alongside siblings Bernadette, Clifford, and Elizabeth. I'm glad our sacred stories are intertwined. And for my two grandmas, Mildred Whitt and Anna Lamb, who taught me the ordinary joy of bedtime cocoa and afternoon card games, it should be written somewhere that I learned a lot about strength and character from each of you.

Last but far from least, to my husband Abe and daughter Isabel, who not only put up with me while I was writing this but did it with grace and cheer: thank you.

Parenting with Hope

The primary goal of parenting, beyond keeping our children safe and loved, is to convey to them a sense that it is possible to be happy in an uncertain world, to give them hope.

—GORDON LIVINGSTON, *Too Soon Old, Too Late Smart*

This book is written in a spirit of hopefulness. I believe we can live well amidst the uncertainties of life and that we can help our children do the same. That said, hope finds its true wings in the winds of doubt and so we could also say this book started in a place of searching.

For the past several years, I've heard an increasing number of parents and grandparents wonder about the kind of world we're leaving to our children. They aren't generally melodramatic people, but it's hard to pay attention to the news and not wonder about where we're headed. I asked a parent the other day, "How are you?" to which they replied, "Other than the existential angst, I'm doing really well." Another parent was prompted into similar reflection after a science update about climate change. "Sometimes I wonder if any of the stuff I've spent my life doing is worth anything. I mean, I've spent my whole career trying to make the world a better place for children and now issues like affordable childcare and educational equality seem futile in the long term," she said.

Sometimes it's healing to hear our own fears voiced aloud. I also wondered how many others were feeling this pressure. In 2017, the American Psychological Association published a report examining the impact of climate change on mental health, concluding that "the tolls on our mental health are far-reaching. They induce stress, depression, and anxiety; strain social and community relationships; and have been linked to increases in aggression, violence, and crime. Children and communities with few resources to deal with the impacts of climate change are those most impacted."[1] Since then, the number of people self-reporting that they experience anxiety about the future of the planet has risen, and that number increases if we include people who have already been directly impacted by the effects of a changing climate. Increasingly severe weather patterns lead to more people experiencing hurricanes, heat waves, and blizzards, which create their own trauma.

And while climate change is posing an unprecedented threat, it's only one of the challenges we parents find ourselves facing. Rapid technology changes mean we don't know what job skills our children will need. Artificial intelligence is either going to save us or destroy us. Safety at school (or the movie theater, or the mall) hasn't been assured since we were kids ourselves, if even then.

This book came out of the questions that are at the root of all of these fears: how do we raise our children in an uncertain world?

There is, of course, our deep desire to make the world a better place for them. I would definitely start there. But chances are, if you picked up this book you're already working that angle. The question that comes next is, "How do we help our children find hope if we can't assure them that everything will be okay?"

It's in solidarity with the deep worry of children and adults alike that I began to look more deeply at the spiritual practices woven throughout Christian history. You know what I mean,

---

1. Susan Clayton, Christie Manning, Kirra Krygsman, Meighen Speiser, "Mental Health and Our Changing Climate: Impacts, Implications, and Guidance," American Psychological Association, Climate for Health, and ecoAmerica, March 2017, https://www.apa.org/news/press/releases/2017/03/mental-health-climate.pdf.

even if the phrase "spiritual practices" is new to you: prayer, generosity, gratitude, Sabbath. I wondered what wisdom they might hold for this time. Were they quaint but archaic practices? Meaningless navel-gazing? Or could they help us shape our lives in a way that would build our sense of hope?

In other words, was there a connection between spirituality and resilience?

What I've found is that this is an area of a growing interest, not only from religious leaders but from mental health professionals, educators, and developmental experts. While religious teachers have been lauding the value of spiritual practices for eons, modern research is now backing that up. Consider Dr. Lisa Miller's research-based book *The Spiritual Child: The New Science on Parenting for Health and Lifelong Thriving*. On her website, she notes that kids with a strong spiritual foundation are less likely to abuse substances, have unprotected sex, or suffer from depression, and they have an increased sense of meaning and purpose.[2]

Often, when I talk to parents about being a Christian parent, they're anxious about answering all of their kids' questions, preventing spiritual suffering, and ensuring that their children stay in the faith. I want all of these things, too, desperately. I want my daughter to grow up with a vibrant, loving faith. No matter what happens to her in life, I want her to be grounded in the idea that God loves her and that her ultimate worth is as a child of God. Ideally, I'd love for her to skip the whole "crisis of faith" stage I went through. But I can't control that any more than I can ensure that she has a great job, a great spouse, and never struggles with anything.

What we can do is give kids the tools they need to navigate life. We can raise them with spiritual practices that will be their

---

2. Lisa Miller, *The Spiritual Child: The New Science on Parenting for Health and Lifelong Thriving* (New York, St. Martin's Press, 2015), accessed May 6, 2019, https://www.lisamillerphd.com/.

anchor when life is hard, or when God seems far away. We can give them a love for exploring and questioning, so that if at some point they're in need of spiritual guidance, they'll know how to search. Of course, the benefit of this is that we'll also be building their spiritual resiliency right now.

The Urgency of the Work

When I began this book, I thought I was preparing for the future. After all, that's how we talk about hope and resilience. They are forward-thinking qualities, so we approach them like they're things we will someday need.

My thinking shifted as the COVID-19 pandemic unfolded around the world. We were thrust into anxiety upon anxiety, at an individual, nationwide, and global level. In terms of learning practices of hope for uncertain times, we aren't just preparing for some eventual take-off, we're building the plane while flying it. While this pandemic will end, life's challenges will continue.

As I finish this book, the novel coronavirus hasn't yet released its hold. I can't speak about the "lessons we've learned" with the authority of a historian looking back at the past. But I can highlight some of the lessons we are learning, with an eye to how they help us understand the role of spirituality in resilience.

It's encouraging to see that almost immediately, people turned to spiritual practices to understand this hard time in their lives. They spoke of the downtime as an opportunity for rest, or Sabbath. They shared the story they were telling with their children. They talked about rediscovering silence as the noise of the world subsided. They reclaimed family mealtimes and rituals that went along with them. They responded with courage and compassion to the needs of their neighbors amidst illness and economic instability.

Hope has both an inward component and an outward one. Practices of resilience help us find courage and trust. They comfort us in times of struggle. But they also inspire us to believe in the vision Jesus gave us, that God's reign will come here on earth. This is why throughout the book I'll highlight the ways that spiritual practices speak to our inner needs. I'll explore how the age-old ways of living answer some of the stresses and anxieties we face today. I'll also explore the issues of justice inherent in these practices.

Family Practices Help Us Learn Together

Several years ago, my friend Sam adopted a child. I remember talking to her just a few months after the adoption was final when she said, "I have so much love for this little person, the fierceness of it scares me sometimes. I understand God's love in a whole new way now. And I also understand how we're supposed to love others, like we're all children." Like so many others before her, Sam had discovered that parenthood can be a spiritual awakening.

Day after day, I hear stories from parents about spiritual lessons their kids have taught them. Preschoolers have a way of opening our eyes to wonder and awe. Elementary school kids are beginning to put language to their experiences. They can talk about beauty and truth in a whole new way. By middle school, the quest for spiritual knowledge is branching out into questions of ethics, theology, and logic. When we engage on this level, we find ourselves challenged to think and rethink how we live. I cannot tell you how many times a family has started coming to church (or, I imagine, other houses of faith) at the urging of their children.

I was a pastor and a teacher before I was a parent. I've had my life transformed time and time again by seeing the world through a child's eyes. Still, when I had my own child, I felt overwhelmed by the desire to "get it right" when it came to teaching her about the faith. I forgot one of the things I'd learned years ago: that I didn't have to bring God to children. Children already experience God. They just need an environment that nurtures their spirituality. In a parenting group for progressive Christians, our covenant became, "Embrace a spirit of play. Invite experimentation. Enjoy questions. Lighten up." Spiritual practices lend themselves to this because the practice itself is the teacher. We don't have to think our way of practicing silence or gratitude is correct. We can just try it and see what happens.

When we keep this in mind, we encourage our children's spirituality with creativity and playfulness. This is important because rituals and rhythms change over our lives. These nine spiritual practices don't have to be done a certain way. Experiment with them. One of the rules I've made for myself is, "whatever works, works."

Spiritual Practices across Religions

Throughout this book, I'll sometimes point out how certain spiritual practices look in other faith traditions. I do this for a few reasons.

The first is because understanding another tradition often helps us understand our own. We gain insight and clarity from seeing what others think and do. I've learned much from my friends and clergy colleagues in other faiths and other denominations. It's a joy to lift up their wisdom in these pages so that it might inspire others.

The second is because spiritual practices can be a unifier across religious differences. My family is mixed-belief, meaning that my husband and I don't share a faith.[3] Some people start out their marriage that way; others may begin in the same faith tradition but one person's faith changes along the way. In either

---

3. The term "mixed-belief" comes from Dale McGowan's book *In Faith and In Doubt: How Religious Believers and Nonbelievers Can Create Strong Marriages and Loving Families* (New York: AMACOM, 2014) and is used here to describe marriages where one person is religious and the other is not.

case, navigating these differences takes a great deal of love and respect. It also means figuring out what you do together as a family and what you do individually.

Connecting the dots between resilience and traditional spiritual practice has helped us align our family practices. Seeing how sacred storytelling can build a foundation of courage for a child has inspired us both to share the stories that are important to us. Reexamining the power of forgiveness has helped us be more intentional about how we practice reconciliation and repair. We might understand the religious significance differently, but we can still participate and learn together. My non-religious husband is much better at practicing both sabbath (meaningful rest) and silence (listening to an internal voice) than I am, even though I have a certain theological understanding about their importance.

I embrace these diverse insights because I believe God's love and grace are big enough to include them. From my Christian lens, I trust that the God I know in Jesus will come to us any way we make room.

The Shape of This Book

This book begins with Sacred Reading practices, where we'll think about the role of story to shape our lives, including biblical stories, family stories, and personal stories. From there, we'll look at Forgiveness. This is the practice that first inspired me to look for the connection between mental health and well-being and spirituality, after a renowned psychologist mentioned that the religious teachings on forgiveness had been foundational in the development of psychology's insights on personal healing.

In the next two practices, Sabbath and Sharing the Table, we'll look at how our daily rhythms of rejuvenation and physical nourishment can offer spiritual nourishment. I was especially intrigued to see the strong connection between these practices and care for the earth.

Our next three practices are also related. We'll begin with Gratitude, a practice that's been well-documented for its mental, physical, and spiritual benefits. Gratitude naturally flows into practices of giving, and so from there we'll turn to Hospitality and Generosity. As we move to Silence, we'll explore our biological need for silence as well as our spiritual need to make space to hear God. Closing with Blessing, a close cousin of prayer, we'll think about how the practice of blessing helps ease our anxieties and builds our faith.

Much is left unsaid in this book. Each time I wrote a chapter, I found myself meticulously narrowing down what I could cover. Without fail, I would finish a chapter and say to my husband, "I could write a whole book about that!" My hope is to help others get started on their own explorations of hope, connection, and resilience. May you find something here to inspire you to embrace play, invite experimentation, and enjoy questions.

A *Blessing for This Journey*

May the path be challenging enough to open you in new ways, and familiar enough to lead you home.

Questions for Group or Personal Reflection

1. How has being a parent, grandparent, or teacher been a spiritual journey for you? What deep truths have you learned from the children in your life?

2. The advice in this introductory chapter is to "Embrace a spirit of play. Invite experimentation. Enjoy questions. Lighten up." Parenting and spirituality are both important, even serious, matters. How do you balance being light-hearted and taking things seriously?

3. Spiritual practices are embodied theology—what we do tells us something about the God we believe in. What qualities of God are you're hoping to explore as you explore these nine spiritual practices?

4. As you think about preparing your children for the world, what is the one trait you most hope they will develop? What gifts, or strengths, do you see in your children already?

CHAPTER 1

Sacred Reading
The Stories We Tell

Stories protect us from chaos.
—BILL BUFORD

Discovering Beautiful Books

When I was about ten years old, my family was on one of our many camping trips in the Colorado backcountry. I had used most of my allotted packing space on books. This time it was *The Chronicles of Narnia*. I can still remember how it felt to finish that series. Perched on a boulder with the fresh mountain air around me, I closed the book and sat there. For a moment the two worlds merged. I was sure I would see Aslan coming over the hill if I just sat long enough. Even as I gradually came back to myself and the real world, I knew that I had been changed somehow.

This was my first experience with what a friend of mine calls "beautiful books." Beautiful books are the ones that affect you on some deeper and often inexplicable level.

Of course, it's not just books that do this for us. Music can do that. Art. Poetry. Movies too, and TV shows. Spiritually inclined people are good at finding these things, so you've probably had these encounters with a story you loved. Sometimes when I finish a particularly beautiful piece of writing, I will find myself sitting there, staring at the words on the page. I'm not reading or thinking or even feeling really; I'm just basking in the experience. Part of what makes them "beautiful" is that they can't adequately be described. If you ask me what *The Chronicles of Narnia* are about, I'd say, "Some kids who go through a magic closet and find a new world." And that wouldn't quite be right, because it sounds so fantastical and irrelevant. So I might try to say, "It's an amazing allegory for the life of faith. And there's a lion who is a Christ figure." This wouldn't sound quite right either because, well, that's booorrrrring. So in the end, I usually just recommend the book and tell the person to find me when they've read it so we can talk about it together.

This is what it's like to try to describe the Bible. Here are things we could say:

- It's the inspired Word of God
- It's a book about God.
- It's a collection of books written over thousands of years.
- It's a series of stories about God's relationship with people.
- It contains history and myth.
- It's the spiritual memoir of how people have understood God in their midst.
- It depicts people at their best and their worst.
- It shows God's constant presence throughout history.
- It demonstrates God's love throughout creation.

None of which quite sum it up, do they? The more we try to nail it down, the more it slips out of our hands. It's what I imagine holding an eel would be like, if I were inclined to hold an eel.

The Bible carries a lot of baggage. While I know a great many people who love the Bible as a holy book, I rarely hear them rave about reading it with the same kind of excitement they express upon reading a fantastic piece of thought-provoking fiction. I suspect it's because the stories seem outdated to us, or we've been victims of a literalist reading that taught us to read the Bible with all the enjoyment of a rule book, or, upon rejecting a literalist view of the Bible, we see only its faults and inconsistencies. Someone once asked me, in a sincere and genuine way, "How can people continue to read the Bible when so many stories depict a god of war, or hate, or at least exclusivism?" They went on to point out that the treatment of women in the Bible often runs from horrific to dismissive, that the Bible has been used as justification for all kinds of "holy wars," and that slavery, antisemitism, and child abuse have all been defended using biblical texts.

Why, indeed, would we continue to say that the Bible should not only be read, but loved? And how do we faithfully read, interpret, and love something that has the potential for such great harm?

Attempting to answer these questions runs the risk of being too simple, or even cliché. They are not questions we should answer once and be done with; we should ask and answer them again and again and again. These questions are the means by which we deepen our faith while also keeping in check our own human potential to bend the Bible to suit our own purposes. So I give the following answer, knowing that it is not complete and that it is, at best, a starting point.

I think of the Bible as a conversation. Just as authors know that their books are a complex interaction between them, their book, and their readers, and that each reader will develop their own separate relationship to the book, the Bible is a multi-directional, multi-faceted, multi-generational conversation. As if that wasn't challenge enough, it's a multi-directional, multi-faceted, multi-generational attempt to describe a people's experience with God. This makes it additionally complicated because the experience of God can never quite be put into words.

The Bible's truth isn't in whether it's historically provable, or whether every story has been rightly interpreted through the ages; it's in the trajectory of the stories together. I once heard someone describe the Bible as the love story of the soul's return to God, a description I love because it hints at the transcendent possibilities within. It is both collective and personal, the story of a people that started out as a tribe then branched into three world religions, as well as the story of us as we figure out how to make sense of the world, God's role, and our own place within it.

TRY THIS: Christians have often tried to explain what the Bible is. They might say, "The Bible is the literal word of God" or "We take the Bible seriously but not literally." Take a few minutes to write down your own ideas about what the Bible is. It's one way to clarify our personal beliefs, but also helpful for talking about the Bible with kids.

The Shape of Our Story

In his book *Bullshit Jobs*, David Graeber looks at the rise in meaningless jobs, the reason for them, and the emotional, mental, physical, and spiritual effect they have on workers. I was struck in particular by his description of the spiritual crisis of "scriptlessness."

Graeber describes scriptlessness as the spiritual challenge of not having a story. For people in meaningless jobs, it happens because there's no way to make sense of their work experience. As a society, we know how to talk about being overworked, we know how to talk about being underpaid, we even know to talk about being undervalued. We don't know how to talk about being bored paper pushers stuck doing who-knows-what all day long.

This lack of meaning is harder to handle—spiritually, mentally, and emotionally—than a job that's hard to do. People in stressful, busy jobs that have a sense of meaning are happier than people doing "sit around all day jobs," even if those "sit around all day jobs" are high-paying.

Graeber's research is about paid work, and it's fascinating. But I want to borrow the idea of scriptlessness to talk about how we're going to keep on doing the hard work of loving the world into a better place. Many of us are, as singer Carrie Newcomer says, "living in the kind of times that ask us to be better people than we ever thought we would need to be."[1]

The reason sacred reading is so powerful is because it reminds us that our job as Christians isn't a scriptless one. We know the story. We know how to live lives of sacrifice and redemption because we have stories of those who have done it before. I don't just mean the biblical accounts, but those of other saints in our world: the Oscar Romeros and Corrie ten Booms and countless others whose stories we know. The job might be hard, but it is meaningful.

There's a passage we often read on All Saints' Sunday, when we celebrate the lives of people who have gone before us:

> Therefore, since we are surrounded by so great a cloud of witnesses, let us also lay aside every weight and the sin that clings so closely, and let us run with perseverance the race that is set before us, looking to Jesus the pioneer and perfecter of our faith, who for the sake of the joy that was set before him endured the cross, disregarding its shame, and has taken his seat at the right hand of the throne of God. (Hebrews 12:1–2)

The biblical stories remind us that although things are hard now, they've been hard before. *Let us also lay aside every weight....*

We're reminded that although sacrifices may be asked of us, they've been asked of others, too. *Who for the sake of the joy that was set before him endured the cross, disregarding its shame....*

Ultimately, we'll remember we don't do any of these difficult things alone. We stand as part of a long tradition of people—that great cloud of witnesses—who found strength and courage just when they needed it.

---

1. Carrie Newcomer, "New Music," accessed October 29, 2018, https://www.carrienewcomer.com/music.

We're going to return to the topic of the Bible and how encountering it as a Beautiful Book can help us live with passion and purpose, even in uncertainty. Before that, though, it's helpful to look more broadly at the role stories play.

TRY THIS: *Some people have a "life scripture," which is a biblical passage or quote that has particular meaning to them. If you already have a passage that's special to you, make a piece of art inspired by the passage. Be creative! This can be painting, collage, poetry, or music, but consider doing something outside the ordinary for you. If you don't have a life scripture, see if you can find a passage that speaks to you today, at this point in your life.*

Family Stories, Sacred Stories

In the picture book *Tell Me a Story Mama* by Angela Johnson, a little girl begs her mother to tell her a story.

"What kind of story, baby?" Mama replies.

"How about the story about when you lived in a little white house, across the field from that mean old lady?" With that, the girl is off and running, telling the story of Mama's childhood all by herself. It's clear she has heard these stories so many times that they have become part of her own life.

Storytelling is universal. It has existed in every known society and continues to play a central role in life around the world today. (Just think of all the money we spend on movies, books, and streaming services!) In an interview with Joseph Sarosy and Silke Rose West, authors of *How to Tell Stories to Children*, they point out that storytelling is how we make meaning.[2] Our brains are uniquely capable of receiving and processing information and ideas through story.

---

2. Joseph Sarosy and Silke Rose West, phone interview with author, May 18, 2020.

This is, after all, why the Bible exists. That it's the story of a family is no coincidence. Beginning with Adam and Eve, continuing through Abraham and Sarah, the much-lauded parents "of many nations" through to King David and then to Jesus, the Bible repeatedly asserts the importance of families and the power of their stories. Two of the four gospels begin with the lineage of Jesus. The point is clear: the family he belonged to mattered, and it mattered because their stories became his story.

Research into the importance of family storytelling has burgeoned. We know now that kids who hear family stories have a greater sense of belonging. The story we tell our children over and over and over again about themselves lets them know they are treasured. I may have rolled my eyes as a child when my mom would regale me with stories about the day I was born, but I also knew how much that day mattered to her.

While storytelling comes pretty naturally and carries many benefits of its own, researchers point out that we can capitalize on their power by thinking about what point we'd like to make with our story.[3] This doesn't mean that we never tell a story for fun, or that every story has to have a morality lesson. It just means that we can help our kids build resilience if we pay attention to whether the stories we tell emphasize the traits we hope they'll have.

My mother-in-law tells a story about a bear wandering into their Alaskan yard when my husband was a toddler. Don't worry, everyone was fine, which is the point of the story. This could be told as a story of sheer luck ("Phew! Weren't we lucky!") or laughed off as a humorous misadventure ("Can you believe

---

3. Sue Shellenbarger, "The Psychological Benefits to Hearing Family Stories This Thanksgiving," interview by Ailsa Chang, *All Things Considered*, NPR, November 26, 2019. Transcript available online at https://www.npr .org/2019/11/26/783069769/the-psychological-benefits-to-hearing-family-stories-this-thanksgiving.

that!?"), or it could be placed within the larger context of hardship and perseverance: "That's what life was like for us then. It was hard and maybe more dangerous than we realized, but we just kept at it and learned so many new things. That hard time it made us stronger." The fact that stories are multi-faceted is exactly what gives them their power. By telling a story rather than giving a lecture, we provide a way for kids to take the inspiration they need at a particular time.

In March of 2020, as the COVID-19 pandemic reached into our world, much was unknown and tensions ran high. In the midst of trying to make decisions about how to continue church services, helping my daughter cope with her school's sudden closure, and wondering about the safety of parents, grandparents, and older loved ones, a welcome email appeared in my box. It was only a few sentences, but it ended with, "This reminds me of the polio quarantines when I was a kid." Politicians, celebrities, and clergy were all doing their best to offer reassurances, but this simple story from someone who had been through it before brought more comfort than the best speech. Even this brief sharing of a personal story called forth courage and calm in a time of anxiety.

TRY THIS: Look through a family photo album with your kids and see what stories emerge.

Writing Is Rewriting: Healing through Storytelling

The mysterious power of a sacred story is how it becomes part of us. We gain courage, identity, and a deeper faith by seeing ourselves as part of a bigger story. What happens, though, when the stories we tell are our own?

This is exactly the question that drives several approaches in narrative therapy, a way of healing that emphasizes the telling and retelling of a painful story. The goal is not simply to tell the story of what happened, but to shift how it's interpreted. For example, a person who was the victim of a crime and now suffers from PTSD might learn to tell the story differently. Instead of emphasizing how alone, helpless, and scared they were, they might also begin to see that they acted bravely, or survived the event, or that despite the ongoing effects of trauma, they've kept their job or remained connected to friends and family. We share hard stories as well as the easy, light, or funny ones because stories of overcoming hardship are how we build resilience.

As writers often remind themselves when faced with an endless slew of edits, "writing is rewriting." No story is complete the first time around, not even the ones we're living. We tell and retell them to make sense of them, and we can choose what parts to emphasize.

In the life of faith, we sometimes do something similar. It's a staple of confirmation and new member classes, seminary programs, and spiritual retreats for people to tell their faith story or answer the question of how has God worked in their life. What's amazing about these stories is that they shift a bit from telling to telling. Sometimes when we look back on our lives, we can see the Spirit at work in different ways.

We sometimes call this a spiritual autobiography, and it also bears a great resemblance to the practice of giving "testimony." Mainline and progressive Christian traditions don't practice this regularly, but if you've been to a worship service where testimony is part of the tradition, you know how powerful they can be. In these moving accounts, people share how God was present at the lowest point of their lives. Recovery from addiction, the death of a loved one, a bout with cancer, or a stint in prison all become opportunities to recognize God's presence. The story is one of transformation, but the story itself is transformative. How it is told shapes how it is understood.

TRY THIS: *Make a faith timeline. You can use pen and paper or create a mixed media version with craft supplies you have* *around the house. Label one end of your timeline "birth" and the other end "now." In between, fill in points in your life that had an impact on your faith.*

The Power of Stories in Difficult Times

From infanthood, my daughter had a pink and black stuffed cow, improbably named "Meowi." Meowi went everywhere with us for years. This included a trip to the children's museum across the state, where Meowi went in for a check-up at the "Be a Vet!" exhibit—and was left behind. Naturally, we discovered our error late that night when we arrived home and faced a bedtime meltdown. No one was going to sleep without Meowi, who was now a four-hour drive away. Without any way to change the reality of the situation, I tried to reframe it by telling a story about Meowi's fantastic adventures in the museum. It didn't stop the heartache instantly, but it did ease it enough that we could eventually sleep.

Stories help us make meaning in difficult times. Kitty O'Meara's poem "And the People Stayed Home," which circulated widely online and was featured in places ranging from O—*The Oprah Magazine* to IrishCentral, retold the story of the COVID-19 pandemic. It was striking because it is set in the imagined future and has a happy ending. It invited us all to reframe the time we were living through as one of healing.

In a similar vein, as children grappled with school closures, loneliness, and anxieties ranging from parental job loss, to fear of getting sick, to increased stress in the household, West and Sarosy started the Coronavirus Storytelling Challenge to inspire parents and kids to tell stories about the virus. As they were clear to state, the goal wasn't to make light of the situation, but to help children and parents cope with it. In short, they were inviting people to participate in transforming their story.

While we might not immediately think of these stories as sacred stories, they, too, open the door to transformation. It's worth noting that meaning-making stories don't have to be great works of art. No one has yet called me to offer an award for a story about a stuffed cow's overnight adventures in a make-believe vet's office. The value is in how the teller and the listener are transformed. When I am tempted to brush off the importance of these little stories, I remember that this is exactly how and why Jesus told stories. Faced with the questions of his followers and detractors alike, he turned to story. Sometimes they were short and pithy, like the parable of the leaven which takes only a few sentences in the Bible. Others were longer with a more developed plotline, like the parable of the prodigal son. Either way, they invited people to wonder alongside Jesus, and to dare to reimagine their lives and possibilities.

TRY THIS: *Journal or draw the story of a challenging time in your life. How did you get through it?*

Talking about the Bible with Kids

My daughter used to attend a Harry Potter reading group. It was organized by Grey Havens, whose mission is to bring philosophy to the public sphere. Each week, a couple of adult facilitators would gather a group of kids around a plain table in an out-of-the-way library meeting room. With simple snacks and some paper for doodling, they'd spend an hour talking about one small part of the series.

I sat in on a few of their gatherings and always left with a mixture of elation and envy. On one hand, I was elated because the conversations were rich and deep—exactly the kinds of conversations I love to have with children. The kids deftly examined questions of morality, meaning, truth, and beauty. Their eyes would light up as they considered whether Snape was a good guy or a bad guy. Was it motive that mattered, or affect? They'd think about the relationship of the wizards and the muggles. Were the magic-users better than the non-magical people? What makes one life more worthwhile than another life?

On the other hand, I was envious because they were talking about things that mattered, using a story for a backdrop, with a passion that I worked hard to elicit in church. Harry Potter, it seemed, was doing better than Jesus. Or, at least the way they encountered Harry Potter was working better than the way we sometimes encounter Jesus.

As I pondered my daughter's Harry Potter group and why it elicited such passion, I solidified my golden rule for reading the Bible: exploration over explanation. Rather than trying to explain the stories, we'd do better to encourage kids to explore them. I gently ask questions like:

- What could this story show us about God? What could it tell us about humans?
- What character seems most like you in this story?
- Why would people put this story in the Bible?
- Where do you see God working in this story?
- What other stories have you heard that are like this one? How is this story different?

In order to do this, adults may have to let go of their need to control the story or its meaning. In a conversation with Laura Alary, author of the beautiful *Read, Wonder, Listen: Stories from the Bible for Young Readers,* she said this well:

> Reading to children is a leap of faith. There is no way to be sure how they will receive what they are hearing. But most children have an instinct for knowing what they need. This is why they often ask for the same stories over and over.
>
> When we share the Bible stories with children, we are inviting them to join a conversation. Sometimes, we'll share a story that doesn't resonate, at least not in that moment. Sometimes, the opposite will happen and they'll

find something beautiful for them that we never could have predicted.

Alary went on to tell this story:

> When my son was about six, he became obsessed with the story of Noah's ark. He wanted to me to read it and tell it repeatedly. He acted it out with his toy ark, and on the couch with stuffed animals and himself in the role of Noah. To make matters more complicated, he also seemed very anxious. One day I found him drawing a picture of what looked like a sandy-colored planet. I asked him about his picture and he said, "This is the earth when it gets too hot and all the water gets used up." Then I understood. He was worrying about climate change and was feeling helpless. I did not say any more, but watched carefully to see what would happen. He continued to retell the story for several days. Then he stopped suddenly and his anxiety went away.
>
> In some way I do not fully understand, the story of Noah functioned as a source of hope and empowerment. By stepping into the role of Noah, my young son gave himself something active to do to save the animals he loved so much. While the story did nothing to diminish the threat of climate change, it brought comfort and consolation to a child who had been feeling overwhelmed.
>
> My point is that while we can choose what stories we tell, and how we tell them, ultimately what children take from them is beyond our control. The best we can do is be observant, and trust that the Spirit is present and at work in the mysterious exchange between child and story.[4]

When people of all ages can place themselves in the context of a larger story, they're able to find a hope that extends beyond themselves. This is a crucial part of meaning-making

---

4. Laura Alary, email interview with author, May 18, 2020.

and being able to live with joy despite whatever immediate, personal threats we face. In order to reap the benefit of this larger story, though, we also have to wrestle with it. That's okay. In fact, I believe it's welcome. Part of the power of storytelling is in the retelling—and reinterpreting.

When Sacred Stories Are Hard Stories

One of the questions parents often ask is how to handle the hard stories in the Bible. It comes up every year before Easter, when we'll be hearing the story of the crucifixion in church. Here's where the dance comes in. First, yes, pay attention to your child's age and developmental capacity just as you would with any story. Be sensitive to the illustrations as well. I wouldn't want gratuitous gore in any movie, TV show, or book.

That said, I also don't advocate completely avoiding the hard stories. In the story of the crucifixion, much of what troubles parents is how they're supposed to make sense of it for their children. Hard stories are made harder when we think we have to make them good or easy. What I model in my own telling of the Easter story, *This Is the Mystery of Easter*, is exploration over explanation, as well as context.

The goodness of a story comes in its breadth. Just as it wouldn't make sense to stop a superhero movie right at the point when the villains have taken over the town, it doesn't make sense to tell our biblical stories as though each one can be isolated from the others. Some of the stories are hard. The good news is that people are still experiencing God at work even in the midst of that hardship.

I was once working with the Noah's ark story with a group of younger elementary school kids. I was hesitant because that story, too, is hard. We might paint our church nurseries with pastel-colored animals happily sailing along, but the destruction of the world at God's hand isn't exactly lighthearted.

I wasn't surprised when one of the kids said, "This doesn't make sense to me. Why would God destroy the whole world?

Why do the animals have to die just because humans weren't good?"

Instead of a lecture on God's sovereignty, or glossing over this question to move onto the happy rainbow part, I asked the kids. "That's a great point. What do you think?" From there, a wonderfully deep and complex conversation emerged, taking into account historical accuracy, how people experience God in hard times, and whether God causes bad things. Then, one kid said, "I think the point of the story is to make us ask this question. That way we can do better than the people in the Bible."

Exploration over explanation.

Trust the stories, the mysterious work of the Spirit, and our children to engage meaningfully with them.

Learning to Love the Bible

When my daughter and I read the Gooney Bird Greene series by Lois Lowery many years ago, we were enamored with Gooney Bird Green's use of underwear as a hat. It's stuck with us. We still laughingly call underwear "two-ponytail hats" when we're folding laundry. We form bonds with and through shared story. The other day I passed a stranger while out walking, and they made a reference to the force of the wind, saying, "We better be careful out here, we'll end up in Oz!" The moment of connection and laughter was deeper somehow than it would have been had we just said, "Wow, it's windy!"

This power is why librarians, teachers, and child development experts emphasize the importance of reading to children in their early years. Campaigns like "1000 Books Before Kindergarten" help parents understand the vital role that early reading plays in the social, emotional, and cognitive development of children. The simple act of reading to children once a day dramatically increases their love of books and their capacity for reading later.

The beauty of doing things together is that it goes both ways. As parents, we also come to love the things our kids love. When we engage in sacred reading with children, rather than "teaching the Bible to them," we make room for the inspiration of the Spirit to work in us, too.

There is a list of Bible stories I now love more because I told them with children. When I was in college, I led a Sunday school class for preschoolers. One morning a particularly precocious child acted out the story of the day using plastic dinosaurs. I never hear the story of Joshua leading the Israelites into the promised land without seeing those dinosaurs, and it always makes me smile. The name of my blog, Barefoot Family, came about because I shared the story of Moses and the burning bush with a group of elementary school kids. Mulling over the story, one kid pointed out that we really should be taking our shoes off at church, like Moses did on the mountain, since church is holy ground. From then on, we took our shoes off whenever we entered the Sunday school classroom.

The best advice I have for helping children love the Bible is to love it with them. Remember that for children and for adults, love comes out in playfulness. Sometimes, it's downright silly (like Joshua and Moses dinosaurs), but it doesn't have to be. Chefs show playfulness when they cook, homemakers play as they create beautiful spaces for living, mathematicians play with numbers as they puzzle over the problem. Play is an open-heartedness with yourself, your subject, and the people with whom you share it.

Adults often think sacred reading is about chipping away at the story like a miner chips away hard layers of rock to get to the gold. It's hard, dirty work and there's very little payoff. If we took a cue from children, we could see ourselves as sculptors instead, still chipping away at marble perhaps, but with the love and passion of artists.

There's a profound truth about sacred stories. They have the power to shape and transform us, but this power primarily comes in relationship. In other words, it's more about who we are than what we do. So rather than trying to "get it right" when it comes to reading the Bible, I approach it with openheartedness. Do it with the spirit of a child.

TRY THIS: *Find a story bible you like and try to read one story a night as a family. I recommend Read, Wonder, Listen by Laura Alary and The Children of God Storybook Bible by Desmond Tutu. The Spark Storybook Bible, edited by Debra Thorpe Hetherington, is another good one, especially for kids early elementary and younger. When you finish, start again. Over time, see how the stories change for each person.*

Contemplative Reading for Adults and Kids

We've come full circle, then, back to reading the Bible. While I believe that a good story bible is worth its weight in gold, the beauty of sacred reading is that there are many other ways to experience stories of faith, for both children and adults. By blending prayer and reading, contemplative practices invite people more deeply into the story. They also remove us from the pressure of reading the Bible "correctly." We're invited to hear the words not only with our heads but with our hearts. This is perhaps why they're attractive to people in all walks of life. Seekers, agnostics, and even atheists have participated willingly in *lectio divina* groups I've led. Children and adults can do imaginative reading together.

Ignatian Imaginative Reading

This practice of imaginative reading comes from Ignatian spirituality. Sometimes called imaginative prayer, or Ignatian contemplation, this method of reading is both prayerful and playful. It is ideal for adults and kids alike, if attention is given to choosing stories appropriate for the age and attention span.

To begin, read the story twice through. The point of these readings is to familiarize yourself with the story. Who is in it? Where is it set? What sounds or smells are present? You might choose to focus on one or two of these elements each reading. If you're doing the reading as a group or a family, switch readers each time. Not only does this keep people engaged, but the different voices are helpful for hearing the story differently.

When you read the passage a third time, you'll be imagining yourself into the story. Try to let go of this process and see if you're drawn to a particular person within the story. If you're doing this alone, you may not need to read the story again. Instead, spend time reconstructing the scene in your mind. Notice what you feel as you watch the scene unfold or take part in it.

If you find yourself drifting into a new place within the story, or not following the steps exactly, that's okay. The goal is to draw nearer to God and to experience the power of story in a new way. As you finish your time with the story, take a moment to sit in quiet prayer or meditation. Share with God what arose for you.

If you're doing this with others, it's interesting to share what you experienced. I'll never forget doing this with a Bible study group as we heard the story of the man whose friends lowered him through the roof of the home where Jesus was teaching (Luke 5:17–39). As we shared our experiences with each other, one person remarked in amazement about the franticness they felt as one of the friends, desperately scouting out a way to get on the roof, and the difficulty of lowering their dear friend carefully down to Jesus. Another imagined the excitement and the helplessness of being the paralytic, hoping against hope that this time there would be a miracle. In our retellings, the story came alive.

Lectio Divina

A second popular way of contemplative reading is called *lectio divina*, meaning "divine reading." It was a monastic practice that traditionally happened in community. Like the Ignatian practice above, it relies on reading a passage through a few times. However, instead of focusing on imagining the people within the story, you're listening for the words themselves. There are many ways to do this. I like to designate something specific to listen for each time.

On the first reading, listen for a word or phrase that jumps out to you. If you're doing this with others, share the words or phrases but don't worry about elaborating or explaining them. Simply share them.

On the second reading, listen for what God is saying to you. Is there a message? A gift? Perhaps simply a reminder of a profound truth you had forgotten? Again, you can share or write down what you received if you'd like.

On the third reading, listen for what God is asking of you. Is there a call to you somewhere? Something you're invited to do, change, or be? As you close your time with this sacred story, spend a moment in prayer. Thank God for the gift or ask for what you need in order to live out the calling you've received.

Florilegium

This last practice is completely different from the previous two, and it works well for groups as well as individuals. At its root, it's simply a book of quotes. It comes from the practice in the medieval church of writing down meaningful sentences while reading the early church leaders. (*Florilegium* means "little flowers." Think of them as bits of beauty you're collecting.)

Originally, these quote books were often kept according to a particular theme. For example, if you were interested in understanding gratitude better, you would write down quotes related to that theme. Eventually, you'd have a whole book of gratitude, with inspiration and insight drawn from many places.

You can also do this with one passage, with a group, or as a family, and have people share the quote that speaks to them.

You can write these down to get a new look at the story or Bible passage through many eyes.

People of all ages find these practices to be relaxing and grounding, and all three practices work well for intergenerational groups to do together, making them ideal for families. These practices emphasize the complex relationship between our bodies, brains, and spirits. Like meditation and prayer, they change the wave patterns in our brains, helping us to become more relaxed and more focused. Because they are scripture-based, they also harness the power of sacred story. The stories become our stories, and even as we transform them in our minds, we are transformed by them.

A Blessing for the Storytellers

May you find the courage to create new futures
by weaving pieces of bright hopes and faded dreams
into guide ropes of new promise.

Questions for Group or Personal Reflection

1. What books have been "beautiful books" for you?
2. Tell or journal about a time you first encountered a story from the Bible that inspired you in some way.
3. When have you found yourself being playful with a Bible story? What could you do to bring more playfulness to your sacred reading?
4. What family stories or "beautiful books" have played a part in your faith life?

References and Resources

Alary, Laura. *Read, Wonder, Listen: Stories from the Bible for Young Listeners.* Kelowna, BC, Canada: Woodlake Publishing, 2016.

Johnson, Angela. *Tell Me a Story, Mama*. London: Orchard Books, 1989.

Renken, Elena. "How Stories Connect and Persuade Us: Unleashing the Brain Power of Narrative." NPR, April 11, 2020. https://www.npr.org/sections/health-shots/2020/04/11/815573198/how-stories-connect-and-persuade-us-unleashing-the-brain-power-of-narrative.

Sarosy, Joseph and Silke Rose West. *How to Tell Stories to Children and Everyone Else Too*. Self-published, 2019.

Shellenbarger, Sue. "The Psychological Benefits to Hearing Family Stories This Thanksgiving." Interview by Ailsa Chang. *All Things Considered*, NPR, November 26, 2019. https://www.npr.org/2019/11/26/783069769/the-psychological-benefits-to-hearing-family-stories-this-thanksgiving.

CHAPTER 2

Forgiveness
Letting Go to Move Forward

Forgiveness does not change the past but it does enlarge the future.
—PAUL BOESE

Discovering Forgiveness

"You hurt my feelings!" The child's voice traveled across the playground as they leveled the accusation at their parent. All of the hurt they were feeling spilled out from their raised voice, clenched hands, and rigid body. I didn't know the details of what had happened, but I knew the experience well. How many times had that scene played out in my own family? I watched as the parent tried to soothe the child, but there was no immediate relief. In that moment, the hurt was simply too deep.

As we look at spiritual practices, one of the things we'll notice is that each practice is rooted in our interconnectedness. Our relationships with each other and our sense of connection with God are among our greatest gifts as humans. The relationships and interconnectedness that can lead to such tremendous beauty and richness are also the sources of some of our deepest pain and struggle. The power of relationships flows both ways. The people we love most are exactly the people we hurt and are hurt by most often—which is why the family is the perfect place to practice reconciliation and forgiveness.

At a lecture hosted by the Interfaith Network on Mental Illness, psychology professor Ken Pargament, Ph.D. noted the great gifts that religious traditions had given psychotherapy. Many of the practices that we now know are helpful to mental well-being were traditionally religious practices. This has been especially true as the field of psychology has expanded to include positive psychology. Positive psychology focuses on strengths and health, rather than illness and cures. In particular, Pargament lifted up the practice of forgiveness. It gives people a framework for releasing the hurt of the past in order to move more fully into the future.[1]

We see this emphasis on forgiveness in Christian teachings like Jesus's well-known instruction to forgive seventy times seven times (Matthew 18:21–22). Other religions also emphasize the value of forgiving even the deepest hurts. In November of 2017 a touching video clip made news. It showed Abdul-Munim Sombat Jitmoud, the father of Salahuddin Jitmoud, who was murdered while delivering pizzas one night. At the trial, Abdul-Munim Sombat Jitmoud embraced Alexander Relford, one of the men convicted in the crime. "I am not angry at you, I forgive you," Abdul-Munim Sombat Jitmoud said in his statement. "Forgiveness is the greatest gift of charity in Islam," he later said.

When I started researching this chapter, I found myself confronting a series of questions on the topic of forgiveness. "Is forgiveness always necessary for healing? What if the perpetrator doesn't ask for forgiveness? How should a person ask for forgiveness? How does the hurting person know if the apology is sincere? Where does justice fit into the picture? If we forgive someone, do we let them off the hook for their wrongdoing? What about repair and forgiveness on the global stage, like the

---

1. Ken Pargament, Ph.D., "Why Spiritually Integrated Psychotherapy Makes Sense: An Evidence-Based Rationale," lecture, May 17, 2018.

work of the Truth and Reconciliation Commission in South Africa that worked to find a way forward for both victims and perpetrators of apartheid? What about the work of racial reconciliation in America? How do we seek forgiveness for layers of injustices?

At first, I found the complexity of these questions overwhelming. What could I hope to say about any of that in one short chapter? Yet, these questions also emphasized the importance of practicing forgiveness at home. If we can't figure out how to negotiate the day-to-day challenges of forgiveness with people we love and trust, how can we be prepared to handle the more complex questions of forgiveness when they arise in the rest of our lives?

These questions point to another reason that forgiveness is hard: we lose sight of the role that forgiveness plays in restoring relationship. In biblical tradition, forgiveness went hand-in-hand with repentance, or "turning around," with the goal of repairing the relationship. One person acknowledges their mistake and tries to fix it, the other person agrees not to seek revenge.

While many people have found the practice of forgiveness to be freeing, even if the other party isn't remorseful, the ideal model for forgiveness is that it happens in the context of a safe and trusting relationship. As we look at the spiritual discipline of forgiveness throughout this chapter, we'll be looking at it through this lens.

TRY THIS: *Make a daily or weekly ritual of checking to see if you're holding onto unforgiven hurts. If so, practice releasing them using the steps at the end of the chapter.*

Forgiveness and Resilience: Finding Freedom

When we talk about forgiveness, it's easy to see why it's good for the person being forgiven. When we have done something hurtful, whether intentionally or unintentionally, the guilt can be overwhelming. We long to be set free from our mistakes. What better way to do that than to repair our relationship with the person we hurt? It's a little harder to define why *giving* forgiveness is beneficial. How does our ability to grant forgiveness affect us and our well-being? To what extent does granting forgiveness allow us to live with more resilience?

For a moment, imagine the last conflict you were in. Maybe it's even one that's current for you: a disagreement with a co-worker or an argument with a sibling or spouse. Now notice the response in your body. If you're really tapping into that moment of conflict, you might be feeling a rush of tension in your arms or a burst of energy in your chest. That's a stress response. Simply by remembering a difficult conversation or hurtful exchange, your body is triggered with a protective flood of hormones designed to help you react in a crisis.

Over time, these physiological reactions might shift. I was angered and hurt by a family member a couple years ago, and I no longer get the same intense flood of emotion when I remember the situation. Instead, it's been replaced with a flash of irritation. If asked, I would say I've gotten over the incident, but in my heart I know I haven't. The irritation I feel is preventing me from being truly open-hearted toward the person involved. It's like the small but ever-present sensation of a pebble that wiggles its way into your shoe when you're out for a walk. It doesn't bother you all the time. Sometimes, you even think it has worked its way back out again. Then, you'll feel its sharp edge and know that it's not gone.

Living with hurt is like that. We can learn to work around it, or do our best to ignore the pain when it comes. Those can be effective strategies, especially in the short term. Ultimately, though, every time we experience the poke and prod of unresolved hurt, we're left a bit more raw. We develop negative thought patterns to cope with the situation. "She acted carelessly" might become, "She's just selfish and can't be trusted." It could even turn into, "Other people can't be trusted" or "I have to stay in control at all times."

Not only are the negative thoughts and feelings painful in and of themselves, they also feed on themselves. We try to protect ourselves from future hurts, but in so doing so, shrink from the world or over-function in it. Both are anxious responses that lead to more anxious responses.

The wisdom of forgiveness is that it gives us a way to transform that negative thinking into a more positive response. We regain a different kind of control than the one our hurt, anger, and protective instincts were urging us toward. We become mentally, spiritually, and physically healthy while also contributing to the overall well-being of the world.

That's why I like this definition of forgiveness from The Greater Good Magazine:

> . . . a conscious, deliberate decision to release feelings of resentment or vengeance toward a person or group who has harmed you, regardless of whether they actually deserve your forgiveness.[2]

Forgiveness helps us transform our pain. As the saying goes, "Hurt people hurt people." By forgiving, we're better able to be the kind of person we want to be.

TRY THIS: *Think of a time you forgave someone. Sit in quiet for a moment remembering what that felt like to let go of the desire for revenge. (Revenge doesn't have to mean that you wanted to hurt them personally, although it can. It might mean that you wanted to see them hurt, or that you wanted to prove to yourself and to them that you were right and they were wrong.) With kids, you can ask them about a time they forgave someone.*

---

2. Greater Good Magazine: Science-Based Insights for a Meaningful Life, "What Is Forgiveness?" accessed May 20, 2020, https://greatergood.berkeley .edu/topic/forgiveness/definition.

When Kids Ask for Forgiveness

In Rosemary Wells's picture book *Yoko's Show and Tell*, little Yoko receives a precious gift from her grandparents in Japan: an antique doll to celebrate *Hinamatsuri*, or Girls' Day. Yoko loves the doll so much, she disobeys Mama and takes the doll to school for Show and Tell. When the doll is broken, Yoko must own up to her dishonesty.

"You have made a bad mistake, my little lotus flower, but I love you as much as ever," Mama replies.

There is a vulnerability that comes from seeking forgiveness. Not only do we have to admit that we made a mistake, we risk rejection when we reach out and try to repair the relationship. Some apologies are not accepted. It takes extra courage to try again, in that relationship or another.

When we talk about forgiveness as a family spiritual practice, it's helpful to start with the parent's role in granting forgiveness. Our kids are going to make many, many mistakes. They'll range from unintentional accidents like hitting a baseball through a window, to misjudgments like the one Yoko makes in the book. Knowing that mistakes, failures, and errors of judgment are part of life; one of the crucial skills of parenting is helping kids repair relationships and move forward themselves after a mistake.

Our response shapes how our kids take responsibility for their own mistakes. Imagine Yoko's story if Mama had responded to her confession, "That was a very bad thing you did. I can't believe you took that doll to school after I told you not to! What were you thinking? When are you going to grow up and take responsibility for your actions? I don't think I can ever trust you again."

It's much easier to see the hurtfulness of this when we look at a fictional character, isn't it? In real life, I know I have said at least some of those things. Harriet Lerner, author of *Why Won't You Apologize*, notes that adults who cannot apologize for their actions likely had parents who responded to their apologies in this way. Rather than accepting an apology, they lectured on the damage the mistake had caused in the first place.[3] They failed to make room for repentance by offering forgiveness.

For some of us, that's because we think that forgiveness, or accepting an apology, means that the topic is closed, that if we say "I forgive you" in the moment when a child is apologizing for taking cookies after being told no, or for riding their bike further than the allowed limits, then the discussion is over and we've let them off the hook. If that's our understanding, then of course we'd use that moment to revisit the damage that's been done. By keeping the bigger picture of relationship and repair in mind, we can use these moments of "repentance" as an opportunity to teach them about repairing a relationship. Making an apology is just one part of that process.

TRY THIS: *Try a breath prayer using the words to the Lord's Prayer. As you breathe in, say, "Forgive us our debts." As you breathe out, say, "As we forgive our debtors." (You can also use "trespasses/those who trespass against us," or "sins/those who sin against us," or another version you prefer.)*

Helping Kids Make Repairs

"Go tell them you're sorry!"

Most parents have said that to their children at some point, often because it's something we heard ourselves when we were growing up. While the idea behind it is good, it's not the most effective way to teach children to ask for or receive forgiveness. Chances are, you've been on one or both sides of this conversation and can predict how it goes:

---

3. Brené Brown, "I'm Sorry: How to Apologize and Why It Matters," interview with Harriet Lerner, *Unlocking Us*, podcast, May 6, 2020, https://brenebrown.com/podcast/harriet-lerner-and-brene-im-sorry-how-to-apologize-why-it-matters/.

"Say you're sorry."

"No!"

"You need to apologize."

"Fine! I'm sorry!"

"Say it like you mean it."

"I'm sorry that you're so mean!"

And so, the battle continues. The focus of the conversation has become the apology itself rather than what led to it. It's little wonder kids soon learn to see "I'm sorry" as some sort of relationship "get out of jail free" card.

While volunteering at my daughter's school one day, I watched one kid say something horrible to another, then rush in with, "I'm sorry! Don't tell Mr. M.! I said I'm sorry!" Obviously, they weren't sorry. Or if they were, they were only sorry about the trouble they were about to be in. The other child, hurt and conflicted, mumbled, "It's okay," and tried to concentrate on their work.

This is one reason that experts recommend parents focus on teaching empathy and making amends instead of requiring a child to say "I'm sorry." The problem with focusing on the apology is that to truly be sorry, a person has to have a solid grasp on empathy. They have to be able to understand that their actions have an effect on others. Since empathy is a developing skill in children, it can be difficult for them to make the many connections between what they did, to how the other person felt, to why they should say "I'm sorry."

On a walk around the park the other day, I saw one young child playing in the sandbox while another was on the swings nearby. Just as the first child carefully scooped sand into a tower shape and declared it a castle, the other child ran over and stepped on the mound of sand, laughing joyfully at the sensation of spraying it everywhere. As Dad came over, he apologized to the child with the broken sandcastle and then turned to his child. "Look, your friend is crying," he said. "She's sad because you stepped on the sandcastle. She worked really hard to make that! Let's help her rebuild it and then you can build your own sandcastle you can smash."

What was so striking in this response is that Dad didn't lecture or shame his little Incredible Hulk-in-training, he simply pointed out what went wrong and showed the child one way to make it right. Nor did he snap that the playdate was over "because you aren't playing nicely" and drag his child home. He stayed with the discomfort of the situation and met both kids where they were.

This is the basic principle behind teaching kids to make amends. It adjusts as they get older and their awareness and skills increase. Parents can then say things like, "Look, she's crying because you stepped on her sandcastle. How could you help fix that?" The apology itself takes a back seat, but the process of seeking forgiveness is still front and center. By the time kids are ready to say "I'm sorry," they understand that "I'm sorry" is a way of expressing regret, not the means of repairing relationships.

TRY THIS: *Books can be a great way to develop empathy because they invite kids to see the world through other people's eyes. Fiction often gives us a clear glimpse into the character's inner thoughts and feelings. Simply by reading with your kids, you're encouraging empathy.4 You can help this along by asking kids about the point of view of characters in the books they're reading: "Why did they decide to do that?" or "I wonder how X felt when Y did this." With pre-readers and early readers, build empathy using picture books by pointing out the expressions on people's faces. One of my favorite books is Hey Little Ant by Phillip and Hannah Hoose. The story unfolds as an ant tries to convince a child not to step on them. The book ends with the*

---

4. Claudia Hammond, "Does Reading Fiction Make Us Better People?" BBC, June 2, 2019, https://www.bbc.com/future/article/20190523-does-reading-fiction-make-us-better-people.

*decision unresolved, making it a great conversation starter for
kids young and old.*

When Parents Apologize

"Okay, but are we ever going to teach kids to apologize? After
all, it's an important skill in itself and it's expected in social situations."

I posed this question to a therapist several years ago when
writing an article for a parenting magazine. Her answer, "Yes,
you're going to teach kids to apologize, just not the way you
think." She pointed out that the best way to teach something is
to model it. I thought of the way my family says "I love you" every
night before bed or throughout the day. We've never demanded
that my daughter say it to us, but she does. She says it because
she's heard it.

The power of this was emphasized in a conversation I once
had with a group of middle schoolers. We were exploring the
story of Jesus and the Canaanite woman from the Gospel of Matthew. Jesus left the city of Gennesaret, where he had been healing and teaching. As he is walking, a Canaanite woman begins
to shout at him, desperately asking him to heal her daughter.
Jesus ignores her. When the disciples ask him to send her away
because her shouting is annoying, he seems to agree. He notes
that he was only sent to bring healing to the house of Israel.
The woman refuses to let that stop her. She runs in front of
him and begs him again to heal her daughter. In the exchange,
Jesus insults her and her people saying, "It's not fair to take the
children's food and give it to the dogs." In other words, "You are
not worthy of my attention." She persists and Jesus eventually
rewards her, saying that due to her great faith, her daughter has
been healed.

It's not the most flattering moment of Jesus's ministry, a
fact the kids picked up on right away. Although some of them
explored one traditional interpretation of the story, which is that

it demonstrates the power of faith, others were quick to note the imbalance of power.

"How humiliating for the woman," one said.

"Well, at least her child gets healed," replied another.

"Yeah, but still. Jesus owed her an apology." This set off laughter.

"Jesus was perfect, he didn't have to apologize," another said.

"Adults never think they have to apologize," came the reply from another youth.

Ouch.

I thought of the many times I'd heard kids describe an unfairness at home or school. There was the elementary school teacher who punished both kids involved in a disagreement, instead of listening to discover that one child really was antagonizing. Or at home, snappy comments made in the heat of the moment were never addressed. I thought of similar moments in my parenting life when I've overreacted or misjudged and let the matter slide rather than apologizing for my own less-than-exemplary behavior.

Adults aren't perfect. So why don't we apologize when we're wrong? Chances are, it's because we think we'll lose our authority by admitting we made a mistake. If our goal is healthy relationships, learning to seek and offer forgiveness is a crucial element of spiritual, physical, and mental well-being.

What makes a good apology? A few things:

1. It names the wrong. We know the importance of this because the lack of this element is exactly what infuriates us with kids' half-hearted apologies. A real apology acknowledges specifically what happened, it's not a general "I'm sorry."

2. It doesn't blame the other person. Not "I'm sorry I yelled at you but you were being so slow!" or "I'm sorry I didn't listen. I was just really frustrated because you were crying." (This is the hardest part for me. When I'm making an apology, I've

learned a golden rule for myself: stop before you want to. Keep it short and sweet.)

3. It offers a way of repair. We can offer a way to fix what happened, or we can explain what we'll do to ensure that it's different next time. "I'm sorry I yelled at you. That wasn't fair. I'm going to work harder at remembering to take deep breaths when I start feeling upset." Or, "I'm sorry I broke your toy. I'll fix it tonight."

TRY THIS: *See what it's like to include confession in your prayer life. Think of it as a way to acknowledge your mistakes within a spirit of love. You can use a simple, "I'm sorry for" or "I wish I hadn't . . ." or you can find a more formal prayer of confession in a book of prayers.*

Accepting an Apology

While visiting a preschool to observe a child one day, I saw an interesting exchange between a teacher and a child. The child misbehaved in some way, which the teacher gently corrected.

"I'm sorry!" the child said.

"I forgive you," the teacher responded.

Slightly taken aback, I looked up from the notes I was making. "I forgive you" seemed like an oddly formal response for a minor mistake. As surprised as I was, I could see the wisdom in the response.

In the United States, our typical cultural response to an apology is, "It's okay."

If our spouse apologizes for forgetting to do the dishes, a child apologizes for leaving their toys out, a stranger apologizes for bumping into us, or a friend apologizes for being late, the answer is always the same. "It's okay."

What's confusing about this reply is that very often, it's not okay. It wasn't okay for Yoko to sneak her doll to school after she was told not to. It's not okay for a preschooler to hit their friend. It's not okay if one spouse is always stuck on clean-up duty. "It's okay" is probably an appropriate response for little things that we'll forget in the next five minutes. A stranger bumping into us or a friend being a few minutes late are "okay." Otherwise, our seeking and receiving of forgiveness will be helped by finding a different way to acknowledge the apology. After all, the apology doesn't make the hurt go away. Instead, it acknowledges that hurt has been done. That's one of the beautiful things about Mama's response in our picture book example. She doesn't hammer Yoko's mistake home to her with a long lecture, but she also doesn't underplay it. She acknowledges both the lapse in judgment and that her love transcends even a big mistake.

Since that observation at the preschool, I've been taking note of other ways to acknowledge an apology. Here are a few I've heard:

- I appreciate your apology.
- Your apology means a lot to me.
- I hear you.
- It will be okay.
- Thank you for your apology.

Like "I forgive you," these responses can sound wooden to our ears. We're used to having our apologies brushed away or the incident overlooked. On an episode of her podcast, researcher Brené Brown noted the same thing while interviewing psychologist Harriet Lerner. They both advocate for the use of "thank you for your apology," but both also point out that this response often makes people uncomfortable. Those words seem to trigger a new defensiveness in people who are apologizing.

I've known this well, having tried to shift from "it's okay" to adopt one of these responses instead. It's not easy. As I think about when I've heard one of these alternative acknowledgments, I realize part of the problem is in tone of voice. Just as someone can say "It's okay" in a tone of voice that implies it's really, truly not, they can say "Thank you for the apology" in a way that says, "I'm going to continue to hold this over you." At home, then, I try to take inspiration from Yoko's Mama, incorporating an "I still love you" or a "We'll work it out together" to my "Thank you for the apology."

Though it's hard to adjust our habitual responses, there are upsides. As a parent, it means that we can accept a child's apology while leaving the door open to help them make amends. If we say, "Thank you for apologizing," and offer a hug when a child breaks a plate, we can follow up with, "Will you help me clean it up?" It also means we can respond sincerely to an apology even when we're not quite ready to move on. I discovered this when a family member apologized for something that I really wasn't ready to forgive. I mulled over their apologetic text for a while, wondering what to say back. I knew we'd eventually reconcile, and I was working on forgiving, but I wasn't there yet. Had I remembered then to say something like, "Thank you for apologizing, I appreciate it," I could have honestly acknowledged the good-hearted and vulnerable attempt at repair while also not feeling like I had to pretend it was okay. In the end, I said nothing, which meant it took us weeks to move past the unsettled feeling in our relationship.

TRY THIS: *Experiment with saying something other than "it's okay" when someone wrongs you. Is there another phrase that would express your true feelings better? Encourage your kids to try it too.*

How to Forgive

Well, here we are.

We've talked about forgiveness and resilience, making amends, giving and accepting an apology, the importance of parental modeling, and we still haven't covered the question that most people ask about forgiveness: How do we actually do it?

As we talked about Judas's betrayal of Jesus one year, one third grader said, "It's hard to forgive a friend when they've done real betrayal. A friend I used to have makes fun of me now. She uses all the secrets I told her back when we were friends against me. I'm not sure I'll ever forgive her."

It's not that we don't believe in it. There are plenty of teachings in the Bible about the importance of forgiveness. Jesus forgives his executioners from the cross, Joseph forgives his brothers for selling him into slavery, the Lord's Prayer contains the line, "forgive us our debts as we forgive our debtors," and Proverbs points out that "love prospers when a fault is forgiven" (17:9, NLT).

When I think back to the first time I truly wrestled with offering forgiveness as an adult, the most vivid memory is the betrayal and hurt that weighed so heavily on my heart. It's like a fog settled in on that time period, cloaking it with anger, frustration, and a feeling of powerlessness. In the midst of that, I remember sitting in church one Sunday morning as the pastor instructed us to pray for our enemies. In that time of silence, I imagined this person in my mind's eye, I pictured them as human and vulnerable and loved by God—and then I choked on the words of blessing. I simply couldn't get my mind to say, "I forgive you, I want what's best for you, I send you blessings." It's an odd and terrible experience to want to do something so badly and yet be unable to do it.

Here's my attempt at putting the big idea of "forgiveness" into some practical steps, using the framework of the spiritual practices we've covered.

Start with gratitude. Think of a time you were forgiven. Be grateful for the spirit and grace that led that person to offer forgiveness. If you appreciate it more deeply now that you're on the other side, recognize that.

Acknowledge the hurt you're feeling now.

Tell the story of the hurt. Some people recommend telling it to someone else, a friend, a pastor, or a counselor. You can walk through it in your mind or journal or draw about it. Whatever you choose, think of it as becoming part of your sacred story. Understanding the role of story, remind yourself that you have the courage to overcome this.

Practice releasing. If you can, release the hurt itself. If not, start where you are. Can you release the desire to see the other person hurt? Can you release some of the anger? Maybe you can release the hesitation to forgive. This is a kindness, a generosity that we give to ourselves and to the other person.

Offer a blessing to the other person. You don't have to see them to do this, you can just send healing or peace their way.

Finally, remember this is a spiritual practice. It might not come the first time. It might even take years, which is perhaps a discouraging thought. It's also an encouraging thought, because it means you're not doing it wrong. You're doing what's hard.

TRY THIS: *Create a forgiveness ritual. Alone or as a family, write something you want to forgive on a small piece of paper. In a candle flame or a backyard firepit, burn the paper as you practice one of the steps of forgiveness. Let it be a symbol of what you've let go of in your quest to forgive.*

A Blessing for Forgiving

May God who walks with us in the giving and forgiving Christ give you courage to repent where you have caused harm, and to forgive the hurts you've borne. And as you practice, may your life shine as a light to all who seek a path of healing.

Questions for Group or Personal Reflection

1. What do you think about the idea that forgiveness is best accompanied by repentance? Are there times to forgive even if the other person hasn't expressed remorse?

2. Is a prayer of confession within your faith experience? What does it mean to apologize to God for something?

3. Think about how apologies were handled in your family of origin. How did that shape you? What would you like to keep or change?

4. What's the most recent occasion for forgiveness you've encountered? (This can be either forgiveness you gave or forgiveness you sought.) How did it resolve?

References and Resources

Brown, Brené. "Harriet Lerner and Brené Brown: I'm Sorry: How to Apologize & Why It Matters." Interview with Harriet Lerner. Podcast audio, May 6, 2020. https://brenebrown.com/podcast/harriet-lerner-and-brene-im-sorry-how-to-apologize-why-it-matters/.

Greater Good Magazine: Science-Based Insights for a Meaningful Life. "What Is Forgiveness?" Accessed May 20, 2020. https://greatergood.berkeley.edu/topic/forgiveness/definition.

Hammond, Claudia. "Does Reading Fiction Make Us Better People?" BBC, June 2, 2019. https://www.bbc.com/future/article/20190523-does-reading-fiction-make-us-better-people.

Pargament, Ken. "Why Spiritually Integrated Psychotherapy Makes Sense: An Evidence-Based Rationale." Lecture, May 17, 2018.

CHAPTER 3

Sabbath

Finding Presence through Our Best Yes

Take rest; a field that has rested gives a bountiful crop.

—OVID

Discovering Sabbath

A lover of all things "old-fashioned" as a child, I read and reread the Laura Ingalls Wilder books. Most of it struck me as idyllic and charming. Getting water from the well? How lovely. Playing ball with an inflated pig's bladder? How quaint. Watching as Ma and Pa stood watch at night while the wolves howled outside? How brave.

My infatuation with their pioneer life was tempered by only one thing: their observance of the Sabbath. I was dismayed by Laura's description of sitting quietly for a whole day. I read with disbelief as she described looking quietly at paper dolls, forbidden even from the quiet creativity of making doll clothes.[1] Thank heavens I was born into a modern family with a spotty record of church attendance; I was free to spend Sundays just like every other day. Longing for a day of rest, as those intrepid

---

1. Laura Ingalls Wilder, *Little House in the Big Woods* (New York: Harper Collins, 1960), 84–85.

pioneers surely did, was completely foreign to me. Where they might have found reprieve, all I saw were endless rules.

I experienced Sabbath in a much different way when I visited a Jewish Renewal congregation several years ago. I'd set up the visit as part of the confirmation class I was leading for middle schoolers.[2] I'd wanted the kids to experience gatherings in other faith communities in order to deepen their understanding and respect for other traditions. I called a rabbi I knew from a local interfaith clergy group, and she enthusiastically encouraged us to come visit.

When we arrived, feeling welcome but a little awkward, we settled in the back and familiarized ourselves with the prayer book. The service began with a reading and a song, and we carefully watched to see when to sit and when to stand. We were following along pretty well until, much to our surprise, the whole congregation turned as one so they were facing the door behind us with smiling faces. Seeing our puzzled faces, the rabbi explained they were welcoming the Sabbath bride. Like an honored guest, Sabbath was ushered in with joyful song. For them, Sabbath was celebration.

This is a better reflection of the biblical idea of Sabbath. The practice of keeping a day of rest as a community is mentioned first in Exodus 16:22. The Israelites, newly freed from slavery in Egypt, were facing the perilous journey to the new land. With no provisions, they relied on mysterious manna in the morning and quail meat in the evening. A day of rest in the middle of the hot desert, with the command not to gather food on that day, must have come as a mixed blessing. While the rest was likely welcome and even physically necessary, the urge to press on to their destination was probably also strong. I imagine the

---

2. Confirmation is a rite practiced in some Christian denominations. It's an opportunity for kids or adults to "confirm" their faith as Christians if they were baptized as babies. It can also mean that the confirmands become official voting members of the congregation.

grumblings of the type-A personalities, the ones with the mental fortitude and physical prowess to walk faster, longer, and harder than the others, complaining about this forced rest. Why slow down when survival is on the line?

Yet, the Sabbath command appears again and again throughout Exodus and Deuteronomy, usually connected with a reminder of their liberation from slavery in Egypt. Sabbath is a gift given by the God who frees people from bondage. The practice of taking time to rest each and every week ensures that God's people will always be anchored in their identity as free people. Never again will they work endlessly for someone else's pleasure. Instead, they celebrate their freedom and the God who grants it.

In that light, Sabbath becomes a revolutionary practice. As Walter Brueggemann says in his book *Sabbath as Resistance: Saying No in a Culture of Now*, Sabbath reminds us that, "You do not need to meet expectations of your mother or your work or your boss or your broker or anybody else. You are free from the quota . . . ."[3]

This is so different from how we often view the idea of rest. Many of us wear busyness as a badge of honor, and we carry the anxiety that goes along with it in our bodies. We seek relaxation with the same frantic pace that drives the rest of our lives. So often I find myself flipping through TV options while surfing the internet and trying to carry on a conversation with a family member. I've heard people say, "Our vacation was jam-packed. I almost need a vacation from my vacation!" Even in our leisure time, we have something to prove.

It's freeing to let go of our striving, worrying tendencies and enjoy the life we have—even if just for a while. For the ancient Hebrew people, and for Jews and Christians who observe Sabbath today, the practice is countercultural. By keeping Sabbath,

---

3. Walter Brueggemann, *Sabbath as Resistance* (Louisville: Westminster John Knox Press, 2014), 46, Kindle.

people proclaim that their identity comes first and foremost from God. All other identities, such as those derived from work or play, are put on hold. For one day, no household chores are undertaken, no food is cooked, no money is earned, nothing is created. For one day a week, the people of God do nothing but remember that they were once slaves but now are free—both as inheritors of a particular faith story and as people who have been freed from the trappings of modern society with its "do more, be more, have more" message. For one day a week, Sabbath invites us to practice just being *enough.*

TRY THIS: *Try a full Sabbath practice for one day. No technology, no work. In what ways is this practice liberating?*

Counteracting Anxiety: Sabbath and Time

"What's the hardest part about being a teacher?"

I posed that question to a group of preschool teachers one day and heard a surprising answer: "lunchtime." While I expected to hear about the challenges of helping kids work through separation anxiety, overbearing parents, or pressure to meet educational standards, what wore many teachers down was the act of getting kids successfully transitioned from their morning activities to lunchtime, then fed and transitioned back to the afternoon.

As I parent, I could relate. Hustling my daughter off to school in the morning is a task I dread. "Get your shoes. *Get your shoes.* **Get your shoes.**" And then, often as not, rounding the corner to find her rolling on the floor with the cat, which she explains quite logically is "part of saying goodbye." Better parents than I have cracked under this pressure.

What adults are experiencing in these moments is often called time pressure. Time pressure is "the psychological stress that results from having to get things done in less time than is needed or desired."[4] This is the mile-long to-do list we all keep in our heads, plus the lists our bosses, clients, and spouses keep for us. Children are equally susceptible to time pressure. When families, schools, childcare programs, and extracurricular activities all have time constraints, children receive a constant barrage of "hurry," "do this now," and "remember, you don't have time to dawdle." When hurry becomes a way of life, it effects our brains, bodies, and spirits. This is the issue at the center of a national conversation about the overscheduling of children. As adults, we know what that constant rush of adrenaline feels like. It's effective for helping us get things done, but it also makes us irritable and eventually exhausted.

That's why learning to rest is a recommended treatment plan for a variety of health struggles, including anxiety. In the book *Natural Relief for Anxiety*, the author recommends this formula for rest as a way of easing the tension of being "on" all the time:

Take a ten-minute break every hour.
Take a one-hour break each day.
Take one full day off per week.

This is practical advice for busy times. It acknowledges the simple fact that our bodies and brains need a break. There is a deeper level, too, that comes from giving ourselves permission to simply be present in the moment.

In the Genesis story of creation, God takes a rest after six days of creating a brand-new world, then declares the seventh day as a holy day. We don't have to take this story literally

---

4. Phil Davis, "What Is Time Pressure and Why Does it Matter?" Towerdata, June 29, 2016, https://www.towerdata.com/blog/what-is-time-pressure#:~:text= Time%20pressure%20is%20a%20type,research%20and%20compare%20less %20criteria.

to see the profound claim that is being made: the world is worth enjoying. More than that, as humans, we are worth celebrating.

While some time pressure is due to having too much to do, some of it comes from an internal sense that we have to measure up in some way. Kids experience this. Even young children express test anxiety as a source of pressure in their lives. The normal but painful jockeying of friends and social groups leads to further self-doubt. Social media adds another layer because adults and kids alike are confronted daily with pictures from friends doing more and having more than them. We know these images are carefully curated to show our best lives, but it's easy to forget that.

In rest, Sabbath invites us to remember who we are. That it is a commandment makes it all the more powerful. We join people over millennia proclaiming that their best version of themselves isn't the working, striving, never-enough version. It's the resting, present, joyful self that God sees, loves, and wants *us* to see and love as well.

As Becky O'Brien, director of food and climate at Hazon, an organization at the forefront of the Jewish Food Movement, says, "You can look at Shabbat and say it's a limitation. You're not allowed to drive. You're not allowed to spend money, you're not allowed to bike, here's all the things you've not allowed to do. Or you could look at it and say, 'This is a day for learning, for connection, for community. This is a day I get to read and study and have phone calls with friends and catch up.'"[5]

TRY THIS: *Make a list of things that bring you joy. How can you incorporate more of these things into your life?*

---

5. Becky O'Brien, video call with the author, May 13, 2020.

Making It Happen: Sabbath for Families

When my daughter was six, we moved across the state, but my job didn't. Weekend after weekend, I would drive several hours to offer an evening service at a lovely little congregation, then drive back again Sunday night or Monday morning. When my daughter got out of school on Monday at noon, all parenting was off. I called those days: "give up being mama days." She'd revel in the forbidden luxury of watching Dinosaur Train until she went cross-eyed and I'd take a nap on the couch. That's pretty much the only "Sabbath" time I can lay claim to in those early days, and honestly, it never felt that spiritual. While we both may have been technically "resting," and I certainly needed that nap, the day lacked any sort of connection with either God or each other.

This is why I feel a little hesitant talking about Sabbath with parents, especially those with younger children. I remember how hard it was to get even a few moments of real rest in the earlier days of parenting. When you have children in the house, getting downtime often comes at the expense of family time.

There's no easy way around the challenge of practicing Sabbath with young children. From my new vantage point, with those all-consuming early years behind me, the wisdom I'd offer would be to remember that life changes quickly. I like the image of "seasons of life" to describe this. Parenting younger children is a particularly demanding season. Children aren't chores that can be set aside for twenty-four hours. Diapers won't wait, sibling arguments have to be resolved, toys will break and need repaired even if we're in the middle of an inspirational Sabbath-friendly read. In that season of life, Sabbath has to look different.

It may be helpful to think about them as two distinct spiritual practices: family Sabbath time to help your kids learn to make Holy Rest, and personal Sabbath time for you to recharge your spirit as well. Family Sabbath might be devoted to family relaxation and fun, which can take a fair amount of work for parents. Personal Sabbath could be the time you make just for yourself. This, too, is a spiritual practice. Even parents need rest and renewal. And when it seems like Sabbath is some distant dream, remember what author Gretchen Rubin so famously said, "The days are long but the years are short."

In our family, Holy Rest has taken a few forms. For a while, we made Sunday "Funday" and took turns picking an activity to do. It wasn't a whole day, it was just one activity. My daughter would choose a trip to the park, I leaned toward family bike rides or walks, and my husband went for outings like miniature golf or ice cream downtown. Whatever we ended up doing, it designated that day as a special time of relaxation and family togetherness. That idea faded from our lives several years ago and morphed into Sunday evening "game nights." I'd set out cheese and crackers and we'd play a board game. In my mind, I wanted this to be something we did for long stretches of time, hours and hours of mirthful game playing. It turns out, I like board games better than anyone else in my family. They can do about an hour before it loses its fun and starts being legalistic. I had to wrestle with a bit of disappointment, but I've come around; whatever works, works.

While my personal pursuit of Sabbath has generally been about creating intentional family time, the simple act of blocking off an afternoon to just be home doing nothing, together, might be even more important. I remember a parent with a large family telling me that their goal was to have two afternoons where the whole family was home together. There was no plan for this time. Sometimes everyone quietly did their own thing puttering around the house, and sometimes someone would initiate an outdoor game or a walk around the city. The practice of simply being home together was enough. Sabbath comes in all forms.

TRY THIS: *With your kids, read the story of Jesus taking a rest in Matthew 14:13–23. In this story, we see Jesus making decisions about when to work and when to rest. Ask your kids how they know when it's time to rest. Share or journal about your own thinking. How do you know when it's time to rest?*

When "No" Means "Yes"

After watching a "Holderness Family" video on YouTube about a "digital diet," my daughter asked if we could try the same thing. The premise is familiar: the family gave up technology for forty-eight hours. No TV, no phones, no computers. I was thrilled. And, since I was researching this chapter on Sabbath, I thought it raised an interesting point: To what extent could we structure Sabbath around certain habits?

When developing a Sabbath practice, the question isn't really "What's allowed on our Sabbath day?" but "What would make rest holy for us?" Laying around the house eating junk and surfing the web on my phone is technically not work, but it's also not restful. Just an hour or two spent like this leaves me irritated and keyed-up, not relaxed and rejuvenated. On the other hand, a long meandering walk around the neighborhood with my family is physically active but also leaves me feeling calmer and more connected with God, nature, and other people.

A friend described their family ritual of cooking dinner together in this same way. For them, it is a pleasant, relaxing way to end the day. In contrast, eating at a restaurant zaps their energy and leaves them feeling rushed. Sabbath activities have a certain quality to them beyond just physical rest—although that's a crucial aspect. Soul rest is an important consideration.

Several years ago, an idea made its way around parenting websites, for parents to give their kids a "yes" day. On yes day, any of the child's requests would be met with "Yes, let's do it!" "Can we have ice cream for breakfast?" Yep! "Can we eat dinner on the living room floor?" Sure! "Will you help me build a LEGO castle?" Absolutely![6]

Parents who tried it said it was liberating for them and their children. For one day, they didn't have to weigh practicality or nutrition or even just making the right decision. Instead, they could reclaim some of their own childlike joy. Who cared if the laundry went unfolded while parents joined kids in a late evening wrestling match on the trampoline? While some parents recommend setting some "yes day" ground rules, most parents report that kids didn't push the limits much. Perhaps because kids are more in tune with their needs for "soul rest," they enjoyed a few forbidden fruits, like extra TV time or a big helping of dessert, but all-in-all, most requests were for simple pleasures like a family pillow fight or a pipe cleaner invention contest.

Sabbath is the ultimate "yes day." It's a day for us to say yes to our souls by doing whatever it is that feeds them. It is an intentional choice to set aside the world for a bit and pursue joy over obligation. Deciding how and when to keep Sabbath is about finding delight in the midst of an otherwise typical week.

I once saw one of those lovely handmade wooden signs that crop up in coffee shops and family rooms. It said, "Life is not measured by the number of breaths we take but by the moments that take our breath away." It's the kind of reminder we desperately need, and yet, no matter how many inspirational plaques we place around the rooms of our homes and our hearts, we struggle to remember. Perhaps this is why the psalmist voiced this prayer: "Teach us to number our days, that we may present to you a heart of wisdom" (Psalm 90:12, NASB).

The practice of keeping Sabbath invites us to pay attention to what really matters. It takes discipline because there are so many

6. Elissa Strauss, "What Happens When You Give Your Kids a 'Yes Day,'" CNN, January 11, 2018, https://www.cnn.com/2018/01/11/health/yes-day-strauss/index.html.

things stacked against it. Remember the definition of "time pressure" I shared earlier? It came from an article about marketing, to help companies figure out how to increase time pressure in order to sell more products. Our human instinct to make decisions more quickly when faced with a sense of urgency is being intentionally manipulated in the pursuit of sales. That's not all that's working against us. Since the industrial revolution, technological advances have led us to value efficiency above other values like quality, sustainability, or relationship and community. Websites, social media apps, and online games are all carefully designed to make us feel like we're missing out if we're not logged on. From notifications to eye-grabbing pictures to the frequent use of red fonts, designers are capitalizing on human nature to grab our attention. It's working; teens spend over seven hours a day on screens, not including usage for school work. Parents fall prey to the same issues, reporting that they frequently feel distracted by their phones.[7]

What this means is that we have to work harder to choose the things that are really important to us. As Ed Cyzewski says in his book *Reconnect*, "The habits and expectations of social media run directly counter to the practices and slow growth processes that make up the bread and butter of spiritual formation."[8] The discipline and invitation of Sabbath is to embrace presence over distraction and slow growth over fast fixes. When this feels overwhelming, I'm reminded that each "no" I choose leads to each true "yes" of life: the people and moments that really matter.

---

7. Lauren Kent, "Try This Smartphone Hack and Other Tricks to Reduce Your Screen Time," CNN, June 11, 2020, https://www.cnn.com/2020/06/11/health/smartphone-hack-reduce-screen-time-wellness/index.html?utm_source=feedburner&utm_medium=feed&utm_campaign=Feed%3A+rss%2Fcnn_health+%28RSS%3A+CNN+-+Health%29

8. Ed Cyzewski, *Reconnect* (Harrisonburg, VA: Herald Press, 2020), Kindle location 266.

TRY THIS: *Keep a time journal for a day. Every time you switch tasks, make a note of what time it is and what task you're doing. What activities are ones you're consciously choosing? What activities are actually distractions?*

Sabbath and the World: Practicing Justice

One of the most thought-provoking questions about Sabbath is to what extent others should pay the price for our rest. If we choose not to cook on Sabbath, is it okay to eat at restaurants or go to a friend's house for dinner? How about having an oh-so-restful spa day? Or hiring someone to come mow the lawn while we watch from the patio with iced tea in hand?

There are different perspectives on this. On one hand, Sabbath is a personal promise and commitment. It's something an individual or family takes on to enrich their own spirituality, not a commitment everyone else is making. In fact, it's not a commitment most people are making. So if I choose to spend my Sabbath at the state park, meaning that my restful time in nature is benefitting from the work that park rangers are doing, I'm not causing harm. They'd be working whether I was there or not.

On the other hand, Sabbath has justice roots. One of the principles of Sabbath is to stand against slavery. Standing against unjust principles isn't just for ourselves; it means taking a stand for others. So while no one is really harmed if I hire someone for household chores on Sunday so I can rest, by violating the spirit of Sabbath, I may be doing a disservice to myself and my own spiritual growth. If part of the Sabbath practice is to shore up our inner resolve to fight the forces of consumerism, production, and perfectionism, then maybe an important part of Holy Rest is that it not come at the expense of anyone else.

I'll admit, this is a daunting idea. For those of us struggling to wrap our heads around a Sabbath day at all, the additional weight of not depending on anyone else's labors seems an insurmountable challenge. The good news is that the question itself is more important than the answer. It's more important that Sabbath prompts us to think about fair and unfair labor than that we resolve the question. Whether you observe Sabbath by going out for dinner or taking the family to the movies isn't the point; the primary issue is, "How will your observance of Sabbath shape your interaction with others?" As your Sabbath practice unfolds, however it unfolds, this is a question I hope you'll consider.

Rhythms of Rest

My daughter's suggestion that we observe a "digital diet" helped me shed some light on the idea of Sabbath. If the goal is to live with more presence, why not just live with more presence? Why not practice being present *every* day? Why not use our phones less *every* day? Why not be more attuned to God *every* day?

Suddenly, the idea of keeping Sabbath struck me as one of those intense diets that people follow. You know the ones; they've come in various iterations over the years, from the cabbage soup diet of the early 2000s to juicing, to Whole 30. The hallmark of all of them is extremely strict rules for a certain amount of time. And every time a new one comes out, the critics say the same thing: these diets don't teach you how to eat well. They're over-the-top, too stringent and will lead to failure. Sure, you might do okay for one week, or even one month, but after that you'll return to your old ways and nothing will have changed.

Is Sabbath like that? Would it be better for us to just integrate all the principles of Holy Rest into our lives throughout all of our days, rather than cramming them into one day?

Actually, I don't think so. There is a benefit to setting up a rhythm of rest, and the diet metaphor is the perfect one to explore if we change our vocabulary slightly. What if, instead of thinking of Sabbath as a crash diet, we think of it as a detox? Maybe our bodies, minds, and souls really do benefit from periodic resetting. If this is true, then developing an intense, all-in practice of Holy Rest might actually help us live more mindfully on the other days.

I've had some success with telling myself to "slow down" or "live in the present." But when I have been most successful is after I've done an intensive brain reshaping, like the silent retreat I took to detox from all the noise in my life. (More on that in the chapter on silence.) Or the attitude adjustment my whole family gets after a week-long vacation. You know the feeling, when you come back and for a little while, you realize that all the stuff you worried about before you left—the household chores, the overgrown lawn, the pile of work on your desk—is not so urgent after all.

A regular experience of Sabbath has the power to shape our hearts and souls. When we immerse ourselves in the experience of being enough, we gradually learn that we can live this way more often. We might still struggle with our to-do lists and our monkey minds, but eventually we'll struggle less.

This is the ultimate goal of Sabbath. That's why it's never been just about the one day of rest; it's about shifting our attitude. Sometimes the best way to shift an attitude isn't to talk ourselves into it, it's to embody it. By living it out, even when it's hard, our attitudes begin to align with our values.

TRY THIS: *Choose a mantra for presence throughout the day. Each time you find yourself feeling pulled into distractions or worries, repeat something to yourself like, "I'm choosing to be present in this moment." "I'm here now, I'll be there later." "The most important thing for me right now is to pay attention." If you already have a centering prayer practice, you could try incorporating a breath prayer throughout the day to draw your attention back to the moment. That might be as simple as "Peace" or "Light of Christ." Anytime you notice yourself distracted or restless, say your mantra or breath prayer.*

Sabbath and the Soul

I've compared Sabbath to a vacation, a "yes day," a digital diet, and a detox. This book, though, is concerned with the spiritual elements of modern life. So what distinguishes Sabbath from other ideas for slowing down and living deeply?

Really, not as much as you'd think. That's why I think this is a spiritual practice whose time has come. Families are crying out for Sabbath time; they're just calling it different things. On an episode of the *Happier* podcast, co-hosts Gretchen Rubin and Elizabeth Craft talked about the importance of a "power down" weekend for families to do nothing.[9] I've recently implemented "no-chores days." Friends of ours are taking mini "staycations" each month.

What separates Sabbath from other observances of rest is the idea that rest can be holy. As we saw in the creation story, rest is part of God's creative process and, as humans, part of ours too. Some of the sacredness of Sabbath comes from remembering the reason we observe it. Often, what distinguishes a spiritual practice from plain old everyday life is a sense of ritual. A routine is something we do repeatedly. A ritual is a routine imbued with spiritual significance.

A few Sabbath rituals I've collected are:

Say a brief blessing for the day at breakfast. This could be as simple as "Thank you God for rest! May we find ourselves renewed by it."

Lock up your household tools for the day. This can be both silly and meaningful for younger kids.

Make a big deal about getting ready for Sabbath. Half of the fun of any celebration is the anticipation. My husband

---

9. Gretchen Rubin, "Podcast 165: Have a Powerdown Weekend," *Happier with Gretchen Rubin*, podcast, April 18, 2018, https://gretchenrubin.com/podcast-episode/165-happier-weekend-liz-dolan.

instituted "Family Planning Group" in our house, which sounds boring but is really a fun way of tackling projects or planning for trips. All it means is that we sit around the coffee table, notebooks in hand, and dream about what we're going to do. There's nothing really magical about it, other than the spirit we bring to it. I drew on this idea to call a "Family Planning Group" session for a day of rest, which led to a grocery list of easy-to-prepare foods and ideas for what we could do. Much like the to-dos of getting ready for Christmas have taken on their own sense of fun, getting ready for Sabbath could be viewed the same way.

If your family doesn't pray regularly at meals, try marking Sabbath by being sure that you pray at one or all of the meals that day.

My family has traditions of lighting candles during holy seasons—Advent, Christmas, Lent, and Easter—so for us, adding a special candle to our Sabbath day has marked it as unique from the other days of the week.

On a similar note, your Sabbath day might be a day a week where you read a Bible story at breakfast or dinner. A devotional, which usually has a brief scripture reading and some reflection, is another possibility. Start or end with a prayer or a blessing. Here are some ideas:

Thank you God for rest! (Short prayers like this are kid-pleasers if everyone says them as loud and as fast as possible.)

"May God bless this day and bless us in it."

Sing "This Is the Day That the LORD Has Made." The lyrics come from Psalm 118 and the tune can easily be found with a quick internet search.

Make a "No work allowed" sign for your front door. You can probably generate some laughs if it says, "God says no working!" Have the kids hang it up at the beginning of your Sabbath time and take it down at the end.

Pair your Sabbath with another spiritual practice you're trying to develop. If your hope is to develop a gratitude practice with your family, make your Sabbath day the day that you share what you're thankful for, or write in your gratitude journal. If you're trying to build more community service into your lives, spend an hour on your Sabbath day working at the food bank, picking up litter, or doing random acts of kindness. These are work, but they're also rejuvenating and emphasize the holiness of both practices.

The point of these ideas isn't to overwhelm. I don't recommend doing them all—that's the opposite of restful! Using any of these rituals can frame your day of rest. Whatever you do doesn't have to be perfect, or even big—in fact, it's often better to start simply and let it grow over time.

TRY THIS: *Think about the celebrations that already have significance for you. Are there elements of those that you can weave into your Sabbath time in order to mark it as a unique and sacred day?*

A *Blessing for the Weary*

When responsibility presses down
like the world on Atlas's shoulders,
may you have the courage to pray
not just for strength to go on but for the wisdom to seek rest.

Questions for Group or Personal Reflection

1. Some activities aren't easily defined as rest or work. What activities help you feel refreshed? What ones make you feel keyed up or restless?

2. What activities are rejuvenating for your family members? Are there differences?
3. How do rhythms of rest, play, and work happen in your life? Do you set aside different times or days for each?
4. Overall, how much of a schedule do you like? Is it more important to you to have a solid routine each day or do you like a lot of flexibility?
5. When are you able to be most present? What makes that possible?

References and Resources

Bourne, Edmund, Arlen Brownstein, and Lorna Garano. *Natural Relief for Anxiety: Complementary Strategies for Easing Fear, Panic and Worry.* Oakland, CA: New Harbinger Publications, 2004.

Brueggemann, Walter. *Sabbath as Resistance.* Louisville: Westminster John Knox Press, 2014.

Cyzewski, Ed. *Reconnect.* Harrisonburg, VA: Herald Press, 2020.

Davis, Phil. "What Is Time Pressure and Why Does It Matter?" June 29, 2016. Towerdata. https://www.towerdata.com/blog/what-is-time-pressure#:~:text=Time%20pressure%20is%20a%20type,research%20and%20compare%20less%20criteria.

Kent, Lauren. "Try This Smartphone Hack and Other Tricks to Reduce Your Screen Time." CNN, June 11, 2020. https://www.cnn.com/2020/06/11/health/smartphone-hack-reduce-screen-time-wellness/index.html?utm_source=feedburner&utm_medium=feed&utm_campaign=Feed%3A+rss%2Fcnn_health+%28RSS%3A+CNN+-+Health%29

Rubin, Gretchen. "Podcast 165: Have a Powerdown Weekend." *Happier with Gretchen Rubin.* Podcast, April 18, 2018. https://gretchenrubin.com/podcast-episode/165-happier-weekend-liz-dolan.

Stafford, Rachel Macy. "Welcome." Handsfreemama.com.

Strauss, Elissa. "What Happens When You Give Your Kids a 'Yes Day.'" CNN, January 11, 2018. https://www.cnn.com/2018/01/11/health/yes-day-strauss/index.html.

Wilder, Laura Ingalls. *Little House in the Big Woods*. New York: Harper Collins, 1960.

CHAPTER 4

Sharing the Table
Nurturing Connection

The shared meal elevates eating from a mechanical process of fueling the body to a ritual of family and community, from the mere animal biology to an act of culture.

—MICHAEL POLLAN

Discovering the Connection Between Food and Spirit

In our house, the practice of family meals waxes and wanes with our schedules. I thought about this one day when, for the fifth night in a row, we'd eaten dinner in the scattered fashion that has become a common part of American life in the twenty-first century.

I picked our daughter up from school at 3:35 and rushed home to feed her a substantial snack. With her lunch period at school only fifteen minutes, she didn't eat very much there. By the time she got home, she was a "hangry" mess. Feeding her something quickly was my secret to survival. It was especially true on nights when she had after-school activities. Our routine was come home, feed Isabel "first dinner," find her leotard or sports uniform or whatever books she needed, then rush back out the door. My husband would come home sometime while we were gone, eat his dinner, and disappear into the basement to squeeze in some exercise. By the time Isabel and I got back home, she was starving again. So she and I ate "second dinner," then got ready for bed. Abe would eventually come back up and eat what was left, usually cold and from whatever pan I cooked it in.

Put mildly, this is not the ideal scenario.

Today's parents have been bombarded with information about the importance of family meals. In a 2015 article for *The Washington Post*, Anne Fishel of The Family Dinner Project catalogued the benefits of eating dinner together. Family meals lead to:

- better eating habits
- a better long-term relationship with food
- better grades
- higher self-esteem
- more resilience to life's hardships
- better relationships between kids and parents[1]

In addition, preschoolers who regularly eat dinner with their family have a better vocabulary, and adolescents who eat dinner together have better moods.[1] Is there anything a family dinner can't fix?

The research into the importance of meals is modern, but the wisdom is not. People have known for eons that eating together makes a difference. We see evidence of that in the many rituals that exist around meals and food. The Jewish tradition has its weekly Shabbat meal, a family dinner that is both meal and prayer. During Ramadan, the days of fasting in the Islamic tradition, Muslims eat together each evening in a celebratory meal called *iftar*. The Sikh tradition includes Langar as a central part of their community. This free meal is open to anyone, regardless of their religious tradition. In many Christian communities, the

---

1. Anne Fishel, "The Most Important Thing You Can Do with Your Kids? Eat Dinner with Them," *The Washington Post*, January 12, 2015, https://www.washingtonpost.com/posteverything/wp/2015/01/12/the-most-important-thing-you-can-do-with-your-kids-eat-dinner-with-them/?utm_term=.9a8b72acf830.

shared meal of communion plays an important role in worship, as we'll explore more later.

The connection between food and spirit is strong. This makes sense, considering the web of labor and nature in every bite we eat. As I type this and drink my coffee, I am connected to the sun that shone on the trees, the soil from which the trees drew nutrients, the rain that fell, and the season through which the trees grew. Mindful eating reminds us that the Divine Spark that is active in all of humanity is active in plants and animals as well.

When I am paying attention, I think of the people who played a part in the production of food: the people who picked the raw coffee cherries, and those who roasted them and removed the pulp, leaving the beans that would later be ground for brewing. I can see in my mind's eye the people who created packaging, the truck drivers, the store managers, and even the clerk who rang up my purchase. With only a brief meditation, I can feel a sense of mystery, wonder, and gratitude over the number of people who played a role in getting me this seemingly simple beverage.

Food is a miracle.

TRY THIS: *As a family, trace a favorite food on its journey to your table. How is it grown or raised? How many hands helped it get to you? Include a prayer of gratitude for each step along the way.*

More Than Fuel

As I pondered the spiritual connections inherent in food, I wondered why it can be such a struggle to make family meals a priority. With all the research about its importance, as well as my sense that food and eating have deep spiritual value, it seems like it should be easier to make a family meal happen more frequently.

A deep dive into the anthropology of food shed some light on the subject. While many cultures have retained a stronger sense of mental, spiritual, or community connection to food, the United States seems to emphasize the bodily aspect of food. Think of those sports drink commercials with taglines like "fuel your life." They show people running, stopping only for a quick pause to slurp down some electrolytes. Protein bars are marketed to everyone from athletes climbing mountains to moms running errands. And while convenience has its place, and sometimes we might need to amp up our electrolyte consumption, the underlying message is that *we're too busy to eat.*

Eating, which can be a source of biological, psychological, social, and spiritual sustenance, has been reduced to an errand akin to filling our cars up with gas. That's an apt metaphor because some food anthropologists argue that it's exactly our industrial and technologically driven lifestyle that shapes our views on food.

The scientific discovery that food is fuel for the body goes back to the nineteenth century when chemist Wilbur Olin Atwater pioneered modern research into nutrition. Thanks to his work, we now understand more about how the body works and how it uses food. Atwater's work also led to a new metaphor—he suggested that food was fuel and compared human bodies to machines.

Following on the heels of the Industrial Revolution, in which people were caught up in a fever of efficiency, this was a powerful idea. Only a few years earlier, this metaphor wouldn't have existed: machines that required fuel were new. Now, though, not only were machines more common, they were highly valued. Food as fuel caught the popular imagination. There's nothing inaccurate about that. Unchecked, though, this metaphor leads us to believe that this is the *only* thing food does, so we lose sight of the other ways that food supports us—biologically, emotionally, socially, and spiritually. When eating is reduced to gaining enough calories needed to get through our day, why not get the calories as efficiently and quickly as possible? But who wants to sit down together to drink a green smoothie?

We can't blame all this on secular attitudes. Religion has contributed its share of poor ideas to our approach to food. Too often, religion has divided the spirit and the body. Texts like Matthew 26:41, ". . . the spirit indeed is willing but the flesh is weak," and 1 John 2:15–17, "Do not love the world or the things in the world. The love of the Father is not in those who love the world . . ." have often led Christians to see things of the body as distractions from things of the spirit. Where food is concerned, holy rhythms of fasting and feasting can easily become rigid. Because spiritual people are concerned with, well, the spirit, it's sometimes hard to develop right-minded teachings around care for the body. To embrace the spirituality of food, we have to reclaim a holistic viewpoint that eschews extremism from both secular and religious sources.

A better approach to cooking and eating emphasizes that we are whole people. Our spirits impact our bodies and vice versa. As Dr. Anil K. Rajvanshi says in a *Huffington Post* article, "Spirituality cannot take place on an empty stomach."[2]

As we embrace the spirituality of food, I'd like to suggest a new metaphor for our consideration. Instead of thinking of food as either fuel for the body or a distraction from the soul, we might focus on the energy of food. I prefer "energy" over "fuel" because it opens the possibility of spiritual, emotional, mental, and physical energy. While we need energy for our bodies to walk, play, and exercise, we also experience energy in countless other ways. We might feel negative energy from a coworker, or positive energy when we're around our spouse. Food, too, contains energy that works on multiple levels. I know that when I eat an apple it's easier for me to experience the spiritual energy of connection to the earth than it is when I drink a powdery protein shake. Since we also talk about things like "divine energy"

2. Anil K. Rajvanshi, "Soul Food: Spirituality and the Enjoyment of Eating," *Huffington Post*, May 9, 2016, https://www.huffingtonpost.in/dr-anil-k-rajvanshi/soul-food-spirituality-and-the-enjoyment-of-eating_a_21465642/.

or "creative energy," we have an awareness that energy works on multiple levels.

TRY THIS: *For one day, pay particular attention to what you eat. The goal isn't to track calories or nutrition, but simply to notice how different foods make you feel spiritually, emotionally, and physically.*

Food as a Spiritual Practice

In the Bible, food plays an important role even for the resurrected Christ and his followers. One of these occasions takes place on the way to Emmaus. As Luke records it (24:13–35), Jesus joins two disciples somewhere along their journey, walking and talking together about the crucifixion and the reports of the resurrection from the woman at the tomb earlier that day. Cleopas and an unnamed disciple don't recognize him even when he spends much of the walk teaching them about the scriptures and interpreting the things that had happened. When they reach their destination, they encourage him to stay with them, concerned about the dangers of traveling alone during the night. Still not recognizing him, they sit down to dinner. Jesus took the bread, blessed it, broke it, and gave it to them. It was in that moment, with the sharing of the bread, that they recognized Jesus. Maybe they remembered all the other times that a meal with Jesus had become a symbol of God's reign among them:

- The feeding of the crowd with only a few loaves of bread and some small fish.
- Jesus's scandalous decision to join the tax collector Zacchaeus for dinner.
- The parable of the banquet that Jesus told one night over dinner, when, after watching his disciples jockey for position, Jesus told of a feast where the most unlikely guests would have the highest honors.

- The Passover supper before Jesus was betrayed, when he gathered with his friends for one last meal and instructed them to remember him in the breaking of the bread.

Jesus's ministry often included food, perhaps because he knew the power of a good meal to both nurture spirits and build bridges. The early church met over a meal, a tradition that has been revived in dinner churches today. Some churches make feeding the hungry a central part of worshipping life, like the Bread Church in Liverpool, England, where people come together to bake bread as part of their worship. Even in traditional Sunday morning services, there are coffee hours after worship, or the well-known and much-loved church potlucks and celebratory fellowship meals.

For Christians, these meals are intertwined with our sacramental act of communion, or Eucharist, in which we celebrate the risen Christ. While there is some variance in the theological understanding of what happens in the sacrament, Christians agree that Christ is made known to us in a unique way in the sharing of the bread and the cup. Because of this, our understanding of God is inseparable from the ordinary act of eating. While this meal stands apart as a sacred meal, it also reminds us that every meal has the potential to connect us more deeply to the God we see revealed in Jesus.

Food Movements: Justice for People and the Planet

In the picture book *The Curious Garden* by Peter Brown, little Liam spends his time exploring his city. Venturing up a dark stairwell one rainy day, he finds a few struggling plants near the remains of an abandoned railroad track. Over the summer, he tends the plants and they gradually begin spreading. A few years later, plants of all kinds have popped up all over the city. "But the most surprising thing that popped up were the new gardeners," the story says as it comes to an end. Colorful pictures show people happily work together to take care of the plants that now cover every inch of the once-barren city.

Brown's book, published in 2009, envisions a way of gardening that has been gaining momentum. Since the early 2000s, the work of food and garden advocates like "Gangsta Gardener" Ron Finley have gained national attention and inspired people to take up gardening even in urban areas. This movement is marked by the twin beliefs that everyone deserves access to healthy food and that anyone can plant something. Finley encourages people to grow food in whatever space they can find, from curbside dirt strips to a few small planters in an apartment kitchen. It is simultaneously an act of beauty and an act of rebellion against fast food and disconnected diets.

Nutrition and health are a driving force in this model of urban gardening. Economics, too, are important. Homegrown food is cheaper than store-bought food, and in food deserts—or food prisons, as Finley calls them—it's a challenge to find fresh food. Finley describes how his own garden came about because he was sick of driving forty-five minutes roundtrip in L.A. traffic just to buy fresh food, despite the fact that California has an ideal growing climate and that neighborhoods like Beverly Hills, fewer than ten miles away, have plenty of access to fresh food.

For other urban and suburban gardeners, sustainability is a key factor in carving out space for a food garden. Edible landscaping has grown alongside other environmentally friendly landscaping trends as people turn their time and natural resources to "food not lawns," as a popular movement proclaims. Some have even taken to calling these home gardens "victory gardens," in keeping with the practice of growing food during the world wars. In this way, food gardening is a practice of creation care, as Christians often call it.

Increasingly, churches and other faith communities are making similar choices, converting underused lots or resource-intensive lawns into food gardens. Sometimes these plots are rented or lent out to community members to grow food as they desire. In other congregations, the produce from the community garden is donated to a local food pantry, meeting the joint missions of serving others and caring for the planet.

In the United States, the intersection of spirituality, food justice, and environmental care is gaining attention due in large part to the Jewish and Christian food movements. Organizations like Hazon, a Jewish organization that "strengthens Jewish life and contributes to a more environmentally sustainable world for all," have been helping people live into the rich traditions of their food and faith. Curious about this relationship for Jews, I spoke to Becky O'Brien, the National Director for Food and Faith at Hazon. She emphasized that the joy that many people find in the work of faith-based food and climate advocacy is the way it connects their day-to-day life, their religion, and their desire to make the world a better place.

> You might think that going to services, and having a bar mitzvah, and lighting Shabbat candles, that that's being Jewish. But for me to realize that going to my local farm stand, eating food in season, growing some of my own food, that's being Jewish. Signing a petition that will lead to legislation that will ensure better care for the earth, that's being Jewish.

She continued:

> The great thing about Hazon is people come to a Hazon conference and their identities are separate. They were a locavore, foodie, restaurant person in one area of their life and a Jew in another area of their life, and now they're in this room where everyone is passionate about both of these things.

Food is the great connector.

Christian tradition, too, is embracing this. Plainsong Farm, founded in 2014, has been one of the leaders in reclaiming the connection between food and spirituality. As they say in their vision statement, "Our ultimate motivation is the belief that pursuing a grace-filled, loving, healthful lifestyle in relation to all of Creation is the most God-honoring way to live."[3]

Gardens might be about nutrition or economics, but they're also about connection with the earth, the community, and with God. As author Thomas Moore says, "The garden reconciles human art and wild nature, hard work and deep pleasure, spiritual practice and the material world. It is a magical place because it is not divided."

It's no wonder that Christian tradition, with its emphasis on the incarnation, or the reconciliation of God and humanity, not only includes eating as central ritual but locates several central stories in a garden. In Genesis, the first encounters between God and humans happens in a garden. The resurrection is first witnessed in a garden. And Revelation, with its vision of Jesus's return in fullness, draws again on the earthy, miraculous imagery of Eden restored to depict the wholeness that is coming.

As I survey my own small yard and the few raised garden beds my husband built, I'm aware of the seemingly small nature of this project. We will, if we're lucky, get a few meals' worth of vegetables. It's a drop in the bucket toward finding a solution to the complex problems woven into our food system.

However, like the urban gardeners I've learned from, I think any steps we take toward reclaiming our connection with food is worth it. This is particularly true for people of faith. The small shifts we make toward appreciating our food, whether by adding a family blessing at meal times or putting some herbs in a sunny window, are also spiritual acts. They emphasize the beauty and the fragility of our earth and of our own bodies. They help us experience and live into the story of a world that is created by God and treasured by humans, rather than a story of a world that is there for our domination or control. Like the curious garden

3. Plainsong Farm and Ministry, "Mission and Values," accessed June 13, 2020, http://plainsongfarm.com/mission-values/.

that took on a life of its own and transformed the whole city, these small, insignificant practices might transform us and grow in ways we can't predict.

TRY THIS: *Grow something unexpected, whether it's a windowsill pot or a new plant in an outdoor garden. No matter whether the experiment is a success or a failure, enjoy the process of seeing what happens. Wonder together what this process might teach us about God.*

Mindful Eating Practices

At the beginning of fourth grade, my daughter's teacher gave her students an unusual writing assignment: a Starburst. Their job was to craft a one-page, nonfiction article about this small candy. Since I volunteered in the classroom, I got a sneak peek at some of the writing pieces.

Kids described the texture of the wrapper, the way one end slightly opened, or how it felt a little bit waxy. They described the shape of the candy in their fingers. There were corners but they weren't sharp. They described, at length, the flavor of their Starburst. "The first little bite I took was melty and the piece stuck to my teeth just a little. It tasted like a mix of lemon and old books." My daughter described how the Starburst felt: "The square was textured and I could feel the small bumps with my tongue." I read this sentence multiple times because until then, I had no idea that Starbursts even had a texture, which is what happens when your only exposure to a food is eating it quickly, often while doing other things.

The Starburst writing assignment wasn't just good for the kids' writing skills, it was a wonderful exercise in mindful eating. Thich Nhat Hanh and Dr. Lilian Cheung describe a similar approach in their book *Savor: Mindful Eating, Mindful Life.* Drawing on an apple as an example, Hanh and Cheung ask readers to hold the apple, see the apple, taste the apple. What is its weight? Its color? Its texture?[7] Their premise is both simple and profound: paying attention to what we eat can create tremendous depth of spirit.

Unfortunately, mindful eating is one of the first things to go when we're busy or stressed, and it's one of the first things we need to reclaim if our food is going to nourish anything more than our basic bodily needs. Even from a nutritional standpoint, mindful eating is important. Diet after diet reminds us of this with words like, "Pay attention to what you eat." The truth is, eating mindlessly is wreaking havoc on our food choices. We eat too much, eat too rushed, make nutrient-poor choices, and treat food as a chore to be accomplished as quickly and painlessly as possible.

Mindful eating helps us integrate our soul and body. Changing *the way* we eat (not just *what* we eat) is like swimming upstream. The factors working against us are no joke. Food manufacturers have a huge stake in making us eat more. They're investing millions of dollars in marketing to cravings, and in developing food that is intentionally addictive. (I'm looking at you, sugar.) Add in our cultural love-hate relationship with food and you have a recipe for an eating disaster.

Aside from all that, mindful eating really comes down to time—which is exactly where this chapter started. In order to eat mindfully, we're going to have to carve out time both for meal planning and for unhurried eating. That means eating at a table rather than at our desk, eating with our families instead of in shifts, and planning ahead so that we aren't scrambling at every mealtime.

After a similar discussion about the importance of family meals with a church group, they brainstormed a list of things that would help them make more time for eating together:

- Plan meals a week at a time.

- Try cooking several meals at once to cut down on cooking time and increase time together at the table.

- Make a "no snacking after 4 p.m." rule so that everyone will be hungry at the same time.
- Stop trying to make dinner together work and have breakfast together instead.
- Host an informal dinner with close friends once a week, to encourage everyone to be home together.
- Dedicate one night a week to "no activities."
- Have a theme for each day, like Taco Tuesday or Meatless Monday, to make planning easier.
- Try new meals because eating the same food each night of the week feels boring.
- Organize the pantry to make it easier to find ingredients.

I offer my own experience and these ideas in part to draw attention to the many ways we can adopt an attitude of mindfulness. But I also offer it as encouragement to keep pressing on as you begin or revamp a spiritual practice. Sometimes the thing getting in our way isn't what we think. Because spiritual practices are embodied practices, they have a spillover effect. Something as simple as deciding to put spirituality at the center of our eating habits might transform our entire way of living. It is both the challenge and the beauty of living more deeply.

Feasting and Fasting: Rhythms of Life

High in a cupboard over our kitchen stove, the kind of cupboard you can barely reach the back of, there's a large yellow plate. It's too big for a dinner plate and too small for a serving plate, which is how it became a birthday plate. I made it at one of those paint-your-own pottery places during a girls' night out with some friends. Honestly, it's not a particularly attractive plate, but it is a treasured one. On it I painstakingly drew a cupcake with a birthday candle, and around the edges borrowed a line from Dr. Seuss's *Birthday Book* to write, "Today you are you, that is truer than true." Three times a year, on each of our birthdays, I stand on tiptoe to dig that plate out of the cupboard and the special birthday person uses it at every meal.

Celebrations like these show how food forms connections and transforms daily life. Our birthday plate is proof of two things: rituals don't have to be complex, and they don't have to be done every day to become meaningful. While I've stressed the power of our daily meals to become moments of mental, physical, and spiritual nourishment, in part due to their frequency, it's also true that our rhythms of life extend past the day-to-day. Weeks, months, seasons, and years all have their own rhythms; building rituals around these days can be another way of expressing and exploring our faith.

The birthday plate reminds me that joy is a spiritual practice. The Bible asks us often to rejoice or be glad. Even while we grapple with the difficulties of the world, as we are also asked to do, we're invited to do it with a spirit of trust and enthusiasm. The word enthusiasm signifies a recognition of being held in God's presence. It comes from two words, *en* (in) and *theo* (God). To be enthusiastic in life is to recognize God's presence within and around us. Celebrations, which developed to mark the most important days of our lives, are occasions to practice enthusiasm. They remind us of the ways God is already present, the everyday and miraculous graces like a baby's birth, and they buoy us for the journey of life.

Another occasion in which Jesus ministered through food came at a wedding, when the hosts ran out of wine much sooner than they'd expected.[4] Not wanting to see them embarrassed, or to have their day of celebration end sooner than it should, Jesus's mother Mary urged him to intervene—and he did, turning water into wine and saving the party. That miracle became a symbol for all the ways that the best is yet to come in the reign of God. But it is also a story of Jesus's presence at a party, with

4. John 2:1–12

food and dancing and wine. It reminds us that God is found in celebration as well as in quiet, that Jesus embraced noisy parties and family meals, even as he also pursued times for rest and individual prayer.

Christians and those of other religious traditions embrace practices of celebration and restraint in food in order to deepen their connection with God. Ramadan marks an important season of fasting for Muslims, balanced each night with a celebratory meal. Jews observe Passover by removing leavening, or yeast, from their homes. For many Christians, Lent, the season before Easter, is a time of fasting. It is book-ended on either side by a festival. Mardi Gras, or Fat Tuesday, was a day of feasting in order to use up the food that wouldn't be allowed during Lent, and had the spiritual and mental effect of preparing people for the days of restraint ahead. Even in Lent, though, Christians have their eye on the feast that is coming: the celebration of Easter.

A friend of mine, part of an evangelical tradition that doesn't observe Lent, was intrigued to hear about this ancient church season. After asking about its meaning and how one could observe it, and being assured that people do things ranging from giving up chocolate, to fasting during the day, to not eating meat on Fridays, as well as a variety of non-food-related practices, she decided to observe Lent by eating simply. She set a few guidelines for herself, things like "no sugar" and "avoid butter and cheese," but for the most part, there weren't strict rules. When Easter came, she said she felt the impact of the celebration more joyfully than she had in years. While it had always had deep spiritual significance for her, connecting it to a bodily practice was invigorating.

Another friend experienced something similar after deciding that the season of Advent, the four weeks leading up to Christmas, would be a time of "fasting." Again, it wasn't a literal fast, but he determined to avoid the Christmas feast foods—like cookies, and eggnog, and other treats—until it was actually Christmas.

Feeling like the steady stream of celebrations that bleed Thanksgiving right into New Year's was actually detracting from his joy, he decided to use food to create a boundary. While it was hard, he too said he felt the beauty of the season in a new way. Advent, the time of preparation and waiting, really was a time of preparation and waiting. And Christmas was marked with renewed celebration and an appreciation for the wisdom of the seasons of life, where we experience celebration and restraint, feasting and fasting, as natural partners.

TRY THIS: *Add a touch of whimsy to a family meal. Have breakfast for dinner or, my favorite, dinner for breakfast. Have a popcorn buffet, eat dessert first, or make a "finger foods only" rule one night. Cultivate joy.*

Food, Comfort, and Crisis

While feasts and fasts are sometimes disciplines we choose, they are also sometimes circumstances we find ourselves in. One of the first realities of the coronavirus pandemic in the spring of 2020 was the run on grocery stores. From cleaning products to dried beans, people begin stocking up. Later, new shopping trends emerged. For several weeks in a row, I couldn't get my usual bag of flour, a staple for our weekend pancakes. My mom texted to say that she hadn't been able to find yeast anywhere, and if it was in stock in my part of the state, could I send her some for Mother's Day? Meanwhile, friends began sharing pictures of their fresh loaves of bread, and several social media groups devoted to "Quarantine Cooking" sprang up.

In our time of crisis, many people were turning to the classic comfort: food. While essential workers were busier than ever, others had more time to spend on traditional arts like bread baking. A few Christian friends began baking their bread for their Sunday morning communion at home. Another friend, part of a denomination that didn't allow for communion to be taken outside the gathered church community, lamented this lost ritual, saying he hadn't realized how much it meant to him until it was gone. From both experiences, people were relearning the connection of food and spirit.

Interestingly, there was another market that quickly became oversold: gardening supplies. There was a practical element to this. As I joined in a Zoom yoga class one Sunday afternoon, the instructor said she'd just finished upcycling a bunch of plastic tubs into garden containers. "My kitchen looks more like a greenhouse," she laughed. "But this experience has taught me the value of self-sufficiency." I empathized. When circumstances feel out of control, anything we can do to be more independent feels good. Even if starting an indoor garden isn't an immediate fix, it gives us some control over the future.

The conversation took a different turn in an online recipe-sharing group. "Bread isn't actually running out at the grocery stores," one woman said. "I'm not making it because I need it, I'm making it because I need to nurture something. Making bread feels like something I can put my energy into and have something good come of it."

Her experience hints at something I suspected. The reclamation of food practices wasn't purely about boredom, or about self-sufficiency, it was about comfort and connection in a time of fear. One reason that mealtimes are so important for building lifelong resilience is that they ground us. The fasts and feasts of our lives become ways we embody our stories. It's why people serve the same foods at holidays as their grandparents served, or why even non-religious people say a blessing at the Thanksgiving table. Food becomes part of who we are, literally, and food rituals shape us spiritually.

My family is mixed-belief. My husband isn't religious, while I, of course, am. Our daughter lives between those two worlds, participating in church life with me on some days, staying home with my husband for lazy Sundays on other days. It's a relationship that has many gifts and a few logistical challenges. The one thing I don't compromise on is a prayer before family meals. This is a commitment I began long before teaching and writing about spiritual practices. I insisted on it because it's how I grew up. My family didn't attend church regularly until I was in high school and felt a calling to be part of a faith community. But we always said prayers before meals and before bed. From those two simple acts, I learned all of the things that I still believe about God today. All of the theological concepts like "incarnation," and "gratitude," and "trust," and "justice for the oppressed," and "love" were taught to me through a few lines of prayer twice a day.

Simple family rituals, mindfully chosen and woven into our day-to-day lives, make a difference. They have the power to be transformative. And when life gets hard, they also have the power to connect us—body, mind, and soul—to the God who sustains all of life.

TRY THIS: *If you don't already say a mealtime prayer, add this ritual to one meal a day. Take turns saying the blessing, or find one prayer you say together every night. Mixed-belief families can find a few examples of non-religious mealtime blessings at ameliadress.com; search "mealtime blessings."*

A Blessing for Your Table

Teach us to be whole in body, mind, and spirit,
so that in our food we find spiritual and physical nourishment.
Fill us with gratitude
for each bit of Creation we find on our plates
and for the hands that brought this holy, ordinary gift to us.

Questions for Group or Personal Reflection

1. What were meals like in your childhood? How does that shape your approach to family meals as a parent?

2. Research and personal experience have shown us that food is an important part of gathering. It's been harder to figure out why shared meals have such significant benefits. Why do you think food is such a powerful bonding experience?

3. Family meals change as a family grows together. How have your mealtimes shifted through the ages and stages of your family's life?

4. Meals play an important part in the Bible as well. What Bible stories about food can you think of? What might these stories teach us about the role food plays in shaping resilience?

5. If meals aren't workable family times for you, how else could you build rituals around food that encourage connection, resilience, and spirituality in your family?

References and Resources

Fishel, Anne. "The Most Important Thing You Can Do with Your Kids? Eat Dinner with Them." *The Washington Post*, January 12, 2015. https://www.washingtonpost.com/posteverything/wp/2015/01/12/the-most-important-thing-you-can-do-with-your-kids-eat-dinner-with-them/?utm_term=.9a8b72acf830.

Rajvanshi, Anil K. "Soul Food: Spirituality and the Enjoyment of Eating." *Huffington Post*, May 9, 2016. https://www.huffington post.in/dr-anil-k-rajvanshi/soul-food-spirituality-and-the-enjoyment-of-eating_a_21465642/.

CHAPTER 5
Gratitude
The Joy of Enough

Gratitude turns what we have into enough.

—AESOP

Discovering Gratitude

"I don't have enough energy for this!"

I was muttering to myself as I scurried through my house, hastily throwing groceries into the fridge. The floor around the kitchen table was covered with tiny purple scraps of construction paper, the counter held the morning's breakfast dishes while the dishwasher held the now-clean but not-yet-put-away dinner dishes from the previous night. It sounds benign in writing, but in truth the chaos was stifling. Where could I even begin to put things in order? There wasn't enough time in the day.

Later that evening I caught myself saying it, and again the next morning, until I began to wonder something semi-profound: How much energy was I wasting on not having energy? What would happen if I said to myself, "This is a lot but I can tackle it?"

Reframing problems can have a tremendous effect on us. A key aspect of developing a growth mindset is to change the language we use. "Problems" become "challenges" for example. "I don't know how to do this" becomes "I don't know how to do this *yet*." The simple addition of a three-letter word completely changes the meaning.

What surprised me was this handy little tip connected to one of my spiritual practices: gratitude. As I practiced paying attention to how much time I had, rather than how busy I was, I found my attitude shifting. I started to be more aware of the gifts of each moment rather than worrying about what the future would bring. Right now, I had groceries to put away and I had the time to do that. I was becoming thankful for what I had rather than bemoaning what I didn't have.

This is one secret of resilient people. A finding of Dr. Robert Emmons, one of the first researchers to examine gratitude, is that grateful people don't necessarily have more good things in their lives. Instead, they reframe what happens to them. Rather than focusing on the negative, they search out the positive. Gratitude amplifies goodness.

In recent years, gratitude has become recognized as one of the keys to happiness and fulfillment. Research into gratitude has boomed, and researchers on the power of gratitude have pointed out that it:

- Enhances empathy
- Increases physical health
- Improves psychological health
- Improves sleep[1]

Spiritual traditions have long stressed its importance. The wisdom of gratitude as a spiritual practice is intertwined with the difference it makes in living well.

TRY THIS: *See if there's a place where you can change your language about a situation. Does it help shift the way you feel?*

---

1. Amy Morin, "7 Scientifically Proven Benefits of Gratitude That Will Motivate You to Give Thanks Year-Round," *Forbes*, November 23, 2013, https://www.forbes.com/sites/amymorin/2014/11/23/7-scientifically-proven-benefits-of-gratitude-that-will-motivate-you-to-give-thanks-year-round/#7d885041183c.

Gratitude As a Spiritual Value

We'll return to the many ways that gratitude makes us a more resilient, hopeful people. But first, it's worth looking at a facet of gratitude that appears often in Christianity and other religious traditions: a recognition of our interdependence. Gratitude reminds us that we are not alone. Once at an interfaith Service of Gratitude, a leader from the local Buddhist Temple explained that in Buddhism, gratitude is connected to integrity:

> The Blessed One said, "Now what is the level of a person of no integrity? A person of no integrity is ungrateful & unthankful."[2]

This quote and the speaker's accompanying teaching helped me see that gratitude isn't just a nice attitude, it's *honesty*. Gratitude is a recognition of all that we have. When we are grateful, we know that we did not earn or are not responsible for much of what we have.

In Christianity, we might say that gratitude puts us in right relationship with God. Consider this passage:

> The one who offers thanksgiving as his sacrifice glorifies me; to one who orders his way rightly I will show the salvation of God! (Psalm 50:23, ESV)

Many of the good things in our lives come down to what some people call circumstances, or luck, and others call grace or blessing. Whatever you call it, there is a humbleness in accepting this, which is an important corrective for our very human tendency to overemphasize our own achievements. Gratitude inspires healthy humility: we are gently and lovingly put in our place.

Perhaps it's this kind of humility and gratitude that inspired the saying, "There but for the grace of God go I," which is attributed

---

2. T. Bhikkhu, "Kataññu Suttas: Gratitude," accessed December 7, 2019, https://www.accesstoinsight.org/tipitaka/an/an02/an02.031.than.html.

to sixteenth-century preacher John Bradford. I first heard it said during a Bible study I was part of in college, along with several people who were older and wiser than me. As the topic turned to addiction and the havoc it can wreak on a family, one man said, "I always try to be as gracious as I can to those who struggle. It's easy to think they simply lack willpower or could get better if they tried, but we don't know the mysterious workings of a person. There's so much circumstance in what kind of life we each get. We shouldn't be too quick to assume we're better than others."

His words have stuck with me, all these years later. I can fall into the temptation to take credit for more than I really earned—as it seems many people do. A powerful example of this comes from a well-known experiment conducted in 2013 at the University of California, Irvine. In the experiment, researchers rigged a series of Monopoly games. At the beginning of the game, one player was given $2,000 and two dice to roll. Each time they passed "GO," that same player would receive $200. The other player was given $1,000 and one die to roll. Each time they passed "GO," they received $100. More importantly, the discrepancy wasn't hidden from the players. Each player knew that the game was arbitrarily rigged. Despite this, players with the advantage consistently exhibited aggressive behavior, coldly taking money from their opponent. By the end, the advantaged players were more likely to attribute their win to skill than to luck. Somehow, they lost sight of the advantage they'd been given from the outset of the game.

I'd argue that this isn't an intellectual mistake but a spiritual one. We probably can't talk ourselves or others into logically understanding the complex ways our lives come together. When we start practicing gratitude, though, the natural effect is for us to become more and more aware of what we have to be grateful for.

TRY THIS: *Make a gratitude list in the style of an awards acceptance speech. (You know the kind, "I'd like to thank the Academy,*

*and my manager, and the other cast members . . . .") Think of
something you've accomplished and make a list of all the people
or circumstances that helped you achieve it.*

Gratitude and Action: Becoming Better People

Keeping in mind what I'd learned about gratitude as honesty, I
wondered whether the outcome of the Monopoly experiment
would be different if players with the advantage were asked to
express gratitude along the way. What if at the moment the
money was doled out, players were reminded to thank the dealer
for the extra money? Or maybe they could simply be given a
poem about gratitude to read and reflect on? Could gratitude
change the way we live as well as how we feel?

Dr. Christina Karns, a researcher at the University of Ore-
gon, completed a two-part experiment to measure this. During
the first part of her experiment, she used an MRI to watch the
brain activity of people while money was transferred into either
their own bank account or the bank account of a food pantry. People who had higher "altruism scores" on a survey experienced more pleasure when the food bank received money.
There was a connection between a spirit of altruism and a spirit
of gratitude. But was it coincidental? More importantly, could
it be changed?

These questions led Karns to a second part of the study in
which participants were asked to keep a journal for three weeks.
Half the participants were assigned the task of keeping a gratitude journal. The other half were asked to keep a journal
but not given any specific guidelines. After the three weeks of
journal keeping, they returned to the lab to repeat the experiment. Once again, Karns monitored brain activity as money was
donated to charity. The result? People who had written in a gratitude journal for three weeks had an increase of activity in the
pleasure center of their brains over their baseline measurement

three weeks ago. In other words, they were happier when money was donated to charity than they had been previously.[3]

The act of being grateful for what they had meant that they felt happier giving to others.

Where plenty of research has demonstrated that gratitude makes people feel happier, Karns's research shows that gratitude also makes us better people. Grateful people aren't just more aware of how much they have, they're more invested in giving to others.

This has real-life significance for people who want to create a better world. Simply by learning to live more gratefully, we can shift the way we take and the way we give. For parents, this is an especially exciting prospect. By teaching children to walk in the wonder of gratitude instead of the fear of scarcity, we might have a real impact on global problems like poverty or food scarcity. What if these issues, which seem so insurmountable for regular people like us, could be solved starting with a change of mindset?

While gratitude has been important to me as a personal practice, the connection between gratitude and generosity motivated me to reclaim it as a family practice. When my daughter was in preschool and had a fascination with cutting and gluing, we made a gratitude jar. We used a cardboard oatmeal canister and collaged it with magazine cutouts of things that brought us joy. Each day we'd write down one thing we were grateful for and drop it into the cannister. That cannister sat on our dining room table for quite a while, until our practice shifted into a ritual of sharing "roses and thorns" at dinner. The idea of roses and thorns is simple: each person names a "rose" from their day, something that made them happy. They also share a "thorn,"

3. Christina Karns, "New Thoughts about Gratitude, Charity, and Our Brains," December 13, 2018, https://www.washingtonpost.com/national/health-science/new-thoughts-about-gratitude-charity-and-our-brains/2018/12/21/238986e6-f808-11e8-8d64-4c79db33382f_story.html.

something hard from their day. Another family we know does this as "three roses and a thorn," and another adds a "bud," something you're looking forward to. One year a church member made beautiful handmade gratitude journals for each child, a practice that many enjoyed, happily showing off their books at the end of the year.

Our practices change and grow as we do. That's the goal of rich, embodied spirituality. Whether you keep a gratitude journal for your whole life or try it for a time before moving on to something else, you're creating a personal and family culture of gratitude.

TRY THIS: *Add a gratitude practice to your family routine. At the dinner table or in the car, whenever you have time, make a game of seeing how many things you can come up with that you're grateful for.*

Gratitude When Times Are Hard

We know gratitude can have a powerful effect on how we experience life. Each day we have a thousand small opportunities for gratitude. Instead of focusing on the unwashed dishes and the energy we don't have, we can choose to pay attention to the fact that the dishes once held food and that we have the ability to tackle them.

What we decide shapes our lives, our happiness, and our spiritual well-being.

There are times, though, when gratitude is much harder than simply reframing life's inevitable challenges. I remember sitting in a hospital room with a patient during my student rotation as a chaplain when she said, "I know I'm supposed to be thankful in all things but I'm having a hard time being thankful right now."

The patient was a young woman struggling to overcome a serious illness. Only one year into seminary, I didn't know nearly enough to be ministering to people in crisis, but I did know this:

you do not have to be thankful when you're lying in a hospital and fighting for your life.

In times of tragedy or crisis, a recommendation to "be grateful" is, at best, something to say when we don't know what to say. At worst, it undermines and overlooks real suffering. I'm not sure gratitude is the realistic response when we're facing cancer or the devastation of a hurricane, or the daily terror of life in a war-torn country. As a pastor, I worry that the Christian emphasis on gratitude might even numb us to the need of our neighbors. I've heard well-meaning and deeply spiritual people make this mistake. Confronted with the plight of Ugandan children carrying water miles every day, they say, "Well, at least they *have* water." Or, to a person facing a terminal diagnosis, "Just be grateful for the time you have left." These responses may be heartfelt attempts to find grace in a situation. Yet, they come across as unsympathetic, quick clichés that relieve our sense of sadness when faced with human suffering. They do little for the person who is hurting.

With this in mind, what do we make of the biblical advice to "give thanks in all circumstances; for this is the will of God in Christ Jesus for you" (1 Thessalonians 5:18) or "Do not worry about anything, but in everything by prayer and supplication with thanksgiving let your requests be made known to God" (Philippians 4:6).

First, it's important to note that the admonishment is not to "be grateful *for* all things." There are many things in life that can't be construed as blessings—not even "blessings in disguise." Acts of terror, violence, natural disasters, persistent poverty, chronic health issues—none of these are blessings. God is not in the business of causing pain and suffering, nor does God expect us to be grateful for these things when they happen.

However, there are times when it's possible for us to retain a spirit of gratitude even in the midst of suffering. We might, with practice and time, be able to recognize grace in other areas of our lives, even when we're facing something hard or downright horrible. In his book *The Spirituality of Gratitude*, which came out of a period of suffering, Joshua Choonmin Kang reminds us, "It is extremely difficult, if not impossible, to be thankful for hardship or tragedy or pain during a crisis." But he goes on to say, "If anyone knows gratitude in that circumstance it is not for the crisis itself, but for God's sovereignty in the midst of suffering."[4] A moment of grace that we might experience within hardship is the simple, quiet awareness that God is with us all the time. This reliance on God in the midst of struggle is one of the gifts and mysteries of faith. There are times in my life when I have been desperate and worried, but the knowledge that "God is still God" has brought a measure of comfort I can't quite explain. Gratitude can center and comfort us, even if it doesn't change the circumstances. I remember a person who, despite a painful chronic illness, managed to remain admirably anchored in the present. "I've learned I can't worry about what's going to happen. I know I'll have good days and bad days and some really bad days. On the good days, I'm just grateful for the good days. The bad days, well, I just try to make it through those any way I can."

TRY THIS: *Use a breath prayer to focus on God's presence. As you slowly breathe in, say, "God is with me." Hold for three seconds, then slowly exhale saying, "God is in the world."*

Gratitude As a Counter-Anxiety Practice

These stories of gratitude in the midst of hardship show us how thankfulness builds resilience. Once we realize that we don't have to be thankful for *all* things, but can still find ourselves grateful for *some* things, we discover that gratitude inspires us to press on in whatever battle we're facing. Gratitude can be like a shield. By protecting us from the desperation that comes when

---

4. Joshua Choonmin Kang, *The Spirituality of Gratitude* (Downers Grove, IL: Intervarsity Press, 2005), 10.

we're faced with trials, gratitude gives us an inner retreat. From there, we can find the courage to keep going.

Holding onto beauty while recognizing pain requires a certain amount of expansiveness. It's a paradox, and humans would often rather resolve a paradox than lean into it. Learning to find hope in grief can help our spirits and our minds.

One example of gratitude in the Bible is the Last Supper. Jesus had come into Jerusalem earlier that day, sent his disciples to the home they'd celebrate Passover in, and somewhere along the way they became aware he was about to be betrayed. By dinnertime Jesus knew he was likely eating his last meal. And yet, ". . . he took a loaf of bread, and when he had given thanks, he broke it and gave it to them, saying, 'This is my body, which is given for you. Do this in remembrance of me.'"

Jesus modeled the paradox of gratitude even in a time of real danger. For him, that food, in those few precious moments with friends, was enough. It wasn't enough forever, it was simply enough for a time.

Sometimes, "enough for now" is really all we have: the moments of laughter that bring a slight reprieve from the chemo, the "I love you" whispered at the bedside of a dying loved one. In those times, we simply grasp the good when we can.

It's hard to live in a time when we don't know what might happen next. We might not feel certain that there's enough to be grateful for in the long term. But we can choose to find enough for any one moment.

TRY THIS: *Make a list of ten things you have enough of for this moment.*

Why Is Gratitude So Hard?

For all of the research on gratitude, not to mention the theological importance and the biblical inspiration, it remains a practice that's hard to implement. In a conversation with a Bible study group, several people mentioned that it's easy to fall into a rut. When they tried to keep a gratitude journal, they wound up listing the same few things every day. "Time with family, laughter, nature, the weather, books . . . my list looks the same every day," one person laughed.

To a certain extent, the difficulty in these practices may be due to things other than our internal capacity for thankfulness. Writing notes requires keeping thank you cards and postage on hand; a gratitude journal requires focus we might not have by the end of the day. But it's also true that allowing ourselves to be grateful can be hard in and of itself.

A friend once told me how reluctant she was to accept help from her neighbors. While she was perfectly happy to *give* help, whether it was taking a meal to the family with the new baby or feeding the cat while her elderly neighbor was away, accepting help was much harder. She paid someone to feed her fish when she left for the weekend rather than ask a friend. Fighting the flu, she insisted to the motherly woman across the hall that she was perfectly fine and didn't need comfort in the form of home-made chicken noodle soup.

"I was happy to give generously," she said, "but it took me a lot longer to learn to accept generosity. I tried to tell myself that I was doing the right thing by not troubling others. Really, I just didn't want to be vulnerable."

There's a vulnerability in letting people do things for us. We in the United States tend to place a high value on independence and self-sufficiency. For some of is, it's downright hard to admit that we can't do everything all by ourselves.

The unvarnished truth is that gratitude is hard on our egos. When we are thankful for something, we are essentially in debt. It's social debt instead of financial debt, but it's debt all the same. One reason we shrug off our neighbor's offer of a hot meal when we're sick is because we don't want to "owe" something. It's the same reason that it's simpler to pay someone to feed your fish than it is to ask your neighbor to check on them once a day. When we pay, we put a concrete value on the task and the transaction is clear. When we ask for a favor, things are murky. There's no way to measure the level of gratitude we should feel—or to know what level of gratitude the neighbor expected. Feeling grateful brings with it a pesky sense of obligation or indebtedness.

Learning to be grateful means losing our sense of self—at least, our sense of a completely independent, self-sufficient self. It slowly chips away at the image of perfection so many of us project. Although saying "thank you" may seem like an easy thing to do, it's actually the slow work of rebuilding ourselves to appreciate the important role of community in our lives.

TRY THIS: *Send a thank you note to someone who is important to you. Be as specific as you can in naming what they did or how they impacted you.*

Gratitude and Kids

Back before I had kids, when I knew everything about being a perfect parent, I always thought I'd avoid the oh-so-cliché parental lecture, "You should be grateful for what you have. Back in my day we didn't [insert topic of argument here]." Imagine my surprise when I found myself saying these exact words one evening at a family dinner out.

I've heard versions of the "you should be grateful for what you have" lecture given by parents in the grocery store and at birthday parties. It's the desperate ploy of a frantic parent, trying to salvage a situation when a child's eager expectations have led to bitter disappointments. When we're rational, we can generally agree that these lectures aren't ideal. If our goal is to raise grateful children, what works?

In my usual parenting post-mortem when a family conversation hasn't gone well, I came up with a couple things I hoped

I'd the remember next time I was tempted to lead with a "back in my day" comment. First, I reminded myself that children don't have the benefit of our years of experience. "Back in my day" discussions aren't helpful for children because they're not relevant. *Everything* was different "back in our day." Cell phones were new, and texting was a big deal. Cars didn't have backup cameras. Houses didn't have solar panels. Hoverboards existed only in cartoons. We can try to convey all these things to our children, but we might as well be describing a fantasy land. When we try to link *our* childhood experiences to things *they* should be grateful for, we're just adding another item to the long list of things that they can't imagine.

This is important from a parenting perspective because it can take some of the defensiveness out of the situation. When a child surveys the presents on Christmas morning and laments that they didn't get the one they'd most hoped for, it's not an attack on the parents. It's simply the disappointment of a kid who doesn't yet know how to focus on what they do have.

In my case, my completely ineffective lecture was triggered by my daughter's disappointment that we wouldn't let her order off the adult menu, when the restaurant offered smaller portions at a considerably cheaper cost on the child's menu. What seemed to me to be the ultimate ungratefulness—pouting over not being able to order a dish too big for her to eat for five times the price—was really a pre-teen feeling the sting of still being considered a "kid." Sure, a saint would have happily accepted their parent's decision with a happy heart. For a real person, though, this would have required the perspective-taking ability of someone much older.

When we're teaching kids gratitude, it's worthwhile for us to keep in mind what we're asking of them. Gratitude is a complex skill, and it takes time to grow into. The "it could be worse" mindset can be helpful for reframing, but it's not a skill that children have naturally.

This is hard for adults, too. Learning to find gratefulness in the midst of disappointment is challenging with a lifetime of practice. Kids might be forgiven for needing some guidance on the journey.

Since we live in an age of instant gratification and immense opportunity, we'd be wise to pay attention to the challenges of staying grateful. It's an ironic twist that the more we have, the harder it is to find something to be grateful for. We suffer from something like diminishing returns on the things we buy or the experiences we have. When we have to work and wait for something we're excited about, we enjoy it more.

Avoiding the entitlement trap often comes down to simplifying life anywhere we can. Making an intentional choice about the things we buy or the activities we do ensures that we are choosing our lives rather than letting consumerism choose them for us. In an interview with Lee Hull Moses, author of *More Than Enough: Living Abundantly in a Culture of Excess*, she recommended taking stock of what you have enough of, what you have too much of, and what you don't have enough of. Honesty, she says, is important for each category.[5] By making decisions based on "what's enough"—rather than "how can I get more?"—we shift our focus to appreciation rather than accumulation. In turn, when we do choose to spend time or money on something, our gratitude and our enjoyment are both increased.

TRY THIS: *In his book,* The Year Without a Purchase: One Family's Quest to Stop Shopping and Start Connecting, *Scott Dannemiller documents his family's renewed connection and deepened sense of gratitude during a year of "no shopping." Try your own challenge by resolving not to shop for a week, or maybe a month. What does it teach you about gratitude, simplicity, and having enough?*

---

5. L. Hull Moses, Skype interview, October 28, 2018.

Gratitude for Parents

A couple of years ago, we experienced our own version of *Homeward Bound*, the movie where a cat and a dog venture cross country to get back home. In our case, it was just one cat and he'd ventured out from a friend's house only a mile away. Still, it took Fizzle three nights to make his way back. During the day, my daughter and I made "missing cat" signs and hung them on doors. At night, I'd prowl through the neighborhood at all hours, flashlight in hand, peering under bushes and calling for him.

I was consumed by worry. The thought of him being out in the world, on his own, without the protection of "his people," was heart-wrenching. Would he know we were looking for him? Did he think we'd abandoned him? Most of all, would he be okay?

It's a bit melodramatic to compare a lost cat to parenthood. There have certainly been times when I've worried about something far more serious to our life and health. But perhaps because it was near my daughter's birthday and the years were inching steadily onward to when she'd be leaving home, I drew comparisons to the challenge of preparing kids to be on their own in the world. For all the work we put in, it ultimately comes down to something that feels like a "sink or swim" situation. Will they have what it takes when they're out on their own?

It took me two nights of no sleep and distracted days, but by the third day of Fizzle's Dramatic Adventure, I realized something. While I was able to find some things to be grateful for—our neighborhood is full of cat lovers who had promised to watch for him, it was late summer so the weather was good, he was the most resourceful of our three cats—it was hard to put a positive spin on the situation.

Instead of trying to downplay my concern, I resolved to spend as much time sitting in gratitude as I spent fretting. I increased my meditation time and focused particularly on experiencing gratitude. By holding one thing I was grateful for in my mind, I could let the feeling of gratitude wash over me, edging out the worry. I didn't have to fight it off, I could just let it drift away.

While cheerful sayings like "Don't worry, be happy" or "Give it to God in prayer" are too unattainable for me to achieve perfect contentment, I could work on achieving a state of balance. "Spend at least as much time in gratitude as you spend in worry" has become one of my guidelines for living well in uncertainty.

TRY THIS: *Think of a time when you were grateful for something. Picture it in your mind and try to feel it again, not just remember it. Practice reclaiming that feeling anytime you can.*

A Gratitude Blessing

May your cup overflow like milk poured by a child's small hand
And when it does, may you see only the gift of having this—
　　a little hand, some milk to pour—
And not the mess it makes.

Questions for Group or Personal Reflection

1. Is it easier for you to make an "enough list" or a "gratitude list"? Why might that be?

2. What do you think prepared Jesus to be able to offer thanks even as he faced death?

3. When have you experienced gratitude in a hard time?

4. The paradox of parenthood is that it's our job to prepare little people for the future while staying present in the moments we have with our children now. What helps you balance looking forward with living in the moment?

References and Resources

Bhikkhu, T. (2000). "Kataññu Suttas: Gratitude." Accessed
  December 7, 2019. https://www.accesstoinsight.org/tipitaka/an/
  an02/an02.031.than.html.
Emmons, Robert. *The Little Book of Gratitude: Create a Life of
  Happiness and Wellbeing by Giving Thanks.* London: Gaia
  Books, Octopus Publishing Group, 2016
Kang, Joshua Choonmin. *The Spirituality of Gratitude.* Downers
  Grove, IL: Intervarsity Press, 2005.
Karns, Christina. "New Thoughts about Gratitude, Charity, and
  Our Brains." *The Washington Post*, December 12, 2018. https://
  www.washingtonpost.com/national/health-science/new-thoughts
  -about-gratitude-charity-and-our-brains/2018/12/21/238986e6-
  f808-11e8-8d64-4e79db33382f_story.html.
Morin, Amy. "7 Scientifically Proven Benefits of Gratitude That
  Will Motivate You to Give Year Round." *Forbes*, November 23,
  2013. https://www.forbes.com/sites/amymorin/2014/11/23/7-
  scientifically-proven-benefits-of-gratitude-that-will-motivate-
  you-to-give-thanks-year-round/#7d885041183c.
Moses, Lee Hull. Skype interview, October 28, 2018.

CHAPTER 6

Hospitality
Welcoming What Comes

True hospitality is welcoming the stranger on her own terms. This kind of hospitality can only be offered by those who've found the center of their lives in their own hearts.

—HENRI NOUWEN

Discovering Hospitality

The picture book *Always Room for One More* paints a compelling picture of hospitality. Based on a Scottish folk song, it tells the story of Lachie MacLachlan who lives in a "wee house in the heather" with his wife and his "bairns to the number of ten."[1]

When a storm comes up one evening, Lachie notes that there's a fire in the fireplace and enough porridge to share, and so he ventures out to flag down every traveler that goes by. "There's room galore. Och, come awa' in. There's room for one more, Always room for one more!" The chorus repeats this way through both the book and the song as Lachie MacLachlan invites person after person into an already-full house.

I've often used this story to talk about hospitality in church communities, because Lachie doesn't simply wait for people to come to him, he's out there eagerly inviting them in. Many United Church of Christ congregations begin worship by say-

---

1. Sorche Nic Leohas, *Always Room for One More* (New York: Henry Holt and Company, 1965), 1.

ing, "No matter who you are or where you are on life's journey, you are welcome here." From Lachie MacLachlan, among other wise theologians, I learned to add, "Not only are you welcome here, you're *wanted* here." Hospitality is the practice of truly valuing others.

It's easy to overlook the radical nature of this practice because we so often confuse hospitality with "entertaining." A friend of mine works in "hospitality management," which means they run a chain of hotels. Restaurants, theme parks, and spas fall under the umbrella of the "hospitality industry" as well. When we think about hospitality in our homes, we might turn to the many magazines, books, and TV shows that guide us to setting the perfect tablescape or making the best dessert.

There's nothing wrong with these practices. I had a colleague who was very good at making any room feel inviting. When we led workshops together, she always thought of the details I'd overlook, like colorful tablecloths to bring cheer to a bare conference room. On our post-workshop evaluations, people would often note that they felt especially welcome and that made it easier to learn new things. But most hospitality comes from the spirit in which we welcome people. Hospitality isn't about being "the hostess with the mostest," it's about growing closer to God by seeing Christ in all people. Hospitality is about welcoming the other.

TRY THIS: *Start where you are with the practice of hospitality. If you rarely have people over, try inviting someone for a simple meal or even coffee. If you love to entertain, consider what small details you might lovingly add to make your guests feel even more at home.*

The Roots of Christian Hospitality

"Car broke down, need money for repairs." The sign was held by a young man standing in the grocery store parking lot, with a woman and child standing near them. It's not uncommon for people to be asking for money on the interstate off-ramps or major intersections, but it's less typical to see people in grocery store parking lots. Nearby there was, indeed, a car that looked like it had seen better days. Through the rear window I glimpsed piles of bedding and household goods. A cross-country move perhaps? Or was their car in fact their home?

I rummaged in my wallet to see if I had cash. I so rarely carry it these days, preferring to pay with debit cards. Coincidentally, this also saves me from having to decide whom to give money to when I encounter these needs. "Sorry, I don't have any money," I can smile and say truthfully, leaving these poor souls and their needs behind me. Today, though, I had the time to look through my purse and found—miracle upon miracle—some bills. I took it over to them and was rewarded with grateful smiles and a heartfelt thank you. "So many people just walk by," the woman said. "We don't know what else to do. We're just trying to get to Utah, where our families live."

What else, indeed? Where does a person turn when they break down in a strange land?

In the Bible, people relied on the kindness of strangers. One story of hospitality is found in Genesis. Abraham was just minding his own business, hanging out near the front of his tent. Looking up, he saw three men standing in front of him.

Abraham didn't waver, wondering if he should help these travelers. Instead, he ran to them and insisted they stay with him. "I'll wash your feet, my wife will make fresh bread, we'll feast on a fatted calf." That's a paraphrase, but even in the biblical story, Abraham's energy and welcome fairly leaps off the page (Genesis 18:5–8). The travelers were not only helped, they were welcomed.

In his book *The Hospitality Commands*, Alexander Strauch points out that in Greek, hospitality is *philoxenia*. This combines the word for love (*phileo*) with the word for stranger (*xenos*).[2] Hospitality, then, can't be misunderstood as simply having friends over; it is intrinsically the practice of treating a stranger like a family member. Hebrews 13:2 calls us back to the story of Abraham with its instruction, "Do not neglect to show hospitality to strangers, for by doing that some have entertained angels without knowing it."

Even the beloved nativity story is one of hospitality, something we are beginning to understand in a new way. We often read it as though Mary and Joseph were cast into the stable "because there was no room for them," an act that sounds distinctly inhospitable. Yet, archeologists have pointed out that in the time of Jesus's birth, the stable wasn't a cold barn, it was likely a room in the house. Animals were kept close by, in an annex of the family home. Biblical scholars have also reexamined the use of the word "inn," noting that it can be translated more like "guestroom."[3]

This means that the story of Jesus being born among strangers in unwelcoming circumstances might not be the key point of the story. Imagine instead a busy city where the house was overcrowded, a relative invited Joseph and Mary into their home, creating space the only way they could. Jesus was welcomed into the world in the most generous way. Perhaps this was even a story he grew up hearing, one of those family stories that shaped how he saw the world and the possibilities inherent in it.

Not only is the Bible full of examples of hospitality, it's full of commands to be hospitable. Over and over again the Old Testament reminds the Hebrew people of their duty to welcome

---

2. Alexander Strauch, *The Hospitality Commands* (Littleton, CO: Lewis and Roth, 1993). Kindle location 390.

3. The same word is used later in the Gospel of Luke, the only gospel that tells of Jesus's birth in an "inn." When it comes up a second time, it's when Jesus celebrates Passover with his disciples in Jerusalem. In that story, it's clear that Jesus knows the person he's staying with and so it gets translated, "guest room."

the stranger and to treat the foreigner as a native born.[4] In his moving cry for God to answer for the tragedies that have been visited on him, Job lists his good deeds, including, "the stranger has not lodged in the street; I have opened my doors to the traveler" (Job 31:32).

These scriptures were written at a time when hospitality was literally a matter of life and death. People undertaking a journey couldn't call ahead to the hotel to reserve a room. They couldn't rely on Google Maps to find a restaurant nearby. If they became sick or an animal was injured, there was no emergency room or twenty-four-hour vet nearby for quick, convenient medical care. Travelers were at the mercy of the elements, luck, and other people.

Then, as now, this was especially true for refugees or people fleeing one land for another. Time after time, the Bible instructs us not just to welcome the traveler, as Abraham did, but to welcome "the foreigner" or "the alien." Where some verses remind us not to "oppress" the alien, others go further, clearly commanding that we take the extra step of welcoming the foreigner. Ezekiel 47:22–23 is just one example of this:

> You shall allot it as an inheritance for yourselves and for the aliens who reside among you and have begotten children among you. They shall be to you as citizens of Israel; with you they shall be allotted an inheritance among the tribes of Israel. In whatever tribe aliens reside, there you shall assign them their inheritance, says the Lord God.

The tradition of hospitality continued into early church practices. First, there was the shared meal around which early Christians gathered and in which all were welcome to participate. Second, the gospel spread through believers who traveled widely and depended on the hospitality of others. Third, the early

---

4. See Leviticus 19:33–34, Exodus 22:21, Deuteronomy 10:19 for examples.

church met in homes of believers.[5] All of these meant that early Christians practiced giving and receiving hospitality regularly.

Ironically, emphasis on Christian hospitality may have led to its decrease as a personal spiritual practice. As people embraced the importance of taking care of those in need, they figured out how to do it more efficiently. Hospitals were opened to care for the sick, especially those who couldn't afford a personal doctor. Hostels provide respite for travelers. Even the words indicate their origin; they share a common root with "hospitality."

It's hard to make a case against these worthy organizations, but it's also true that the virtue of hospitality soon gave way to the business of hospitality, and eventually hospitality lost its personal connection. For us to reclaim it, let's consider why and how it still matters today.

TRY THIS: *Think about how you could extend hospitality to a stranger. What practice could you take on to better connect you to "the other"?*

Learning by Receiving

Several years ago, I found myself sitting at a table in a large Catholic church, looking around with both curiosity and trepidation. I was there for a meeting of their moms' group.

I went because my neighbor invited me and she seemed nice, which was enough, because I was new to the area and desperate for friends. Peering through my front windows, anxiously waiting for a neighbor to emerge into our suburban cul-de-sac so I could "just happen" to wander outside, is a slow way to meet people.

"I'll go for a few meetings," I told my husband before I left. "At least I'll get out of the house for a bit."

---

5. Strauch, *The Hospitality Commands*, 413.

My hesitation about the group wasn't completely unfounded. It was, after all, a group of mostly Catholic women and I am a female Protestant pastor. No one else seemed to care, but I was acutely aware that I didn't belong in the same way they did.

My best efforts to not get too involved with the group ended when they began the practice of sharing prayer requests. "I'm grateful that my daughter is settling in well at school," I said cheerily. Everyone smiled encouragingly and nodded.

I got by with variations on that theme for the next couple weeks until a crisis hit my extended family. That night at our meeting, without even meaning to, I blurted out the entire story. Then I cried. Then I left and felt like an idiot. The old me, in the old location, would never have shared this kind of information with people I was just meeting. But this was the vulnerable me, the one who had to accept invitations from strangers and who gratefully accepted help from wherever it might come.

Sometimes we learn hospitality by receiving it, something the Bible reminds us in passages like Deuteronomy 10:19 where it says, "You shall also love the stranger, for you were strangers in the land of Egypt." Because I was once invited to a group by a person I barely knew, and because I once took comfort and strength from women who were not like me at all, I learned more about the life-changing power of hospitality.

Loneliness, a rising problem in the United States, contributes to a host of physical and mental health issues. According to the UnLonely Project, loneliness increases anxiety and depression. Due to its effects on physical and mental health, it's as lethal as smoking fifteen cigarettes a day. It also affects certain age groups more than others: teens, young adults, and older adults face higher risks of loneliness and consequences from its effects.[6]

---

6. The UnLonely Project, "Fact Sheet: Loneliness and Isolation," accessed May 11, 2020, https://artandhealing.org/isolation-and-loneliness-fact-sheet/?gclid=CjwKCAjw7-P1BRA2EiwAXoPWAyoE2maJBhdJEwJUSqiLuZ60MFbZ-Z0HYtzDR5_S4iqArG8exdEJfhoC9n4QAvD_BwE.

I ended up staying with that group for several months, until work commitments got in the way. The neighbor who invited me to that group has since moved, but I ran into her recently and told her what a difference the invitation had made. "Really?" she asked. "I kind of felt silly. I thought everyone knew that they could just go anytime. I worried you'd think I was being pushy." There are so many things that are, in theory, "open to all." Churches. Library programs. Town gatherings. Neighborhood get-togethers. An apartment building that we once lived in held weekly social gatherings that no one came to except my husband, myself, and a father and son from three floors down. I assumed then that it was busyness, or worse, snobbery, but maybe not. Maybe we are all fighting off the insecurity that "everyone is welcome!" means, "everyone who has it all together is welcome!"

As I look back on that experience, I wonder why if my insistence on being the perfect guest, cheerful, helpful, and presentable, is part of a larger cultural challenge. Maybe part of the reason we're so lonely as a nation is because we're afraid to be dependent on others. If so, part of the rising anxiety with an uncertain world is admitting that we can't go it alone. We have to shed the layers of independence we've so carefully cultivated and lean more deeply into the idea that we really are connected. Learning to accept hospitality as well as to give, is one step toward a better world as well as higher resilience.

TRY THIS: *Think of something you attend (church, a class, story time at the library) that someone else might enjoy. Practice inviting a new friend or neighbor to go with you.*

Hospitality Bridges Divides

My moms' group experience hints at another challenge to our collective physical and mental well-being: tribalism, or our ever-shrinking bubbles of comfort. We can become insular in our geographic groups, our religious identities, or our races and economic classes. It's well-documented that our society is increasingly fragmented and that much of it is due to political tension. Tribalism refers to our human penchant for creating insular groups for ourselves. It's a natural enough instinct; for millions of years, humans lived in tribes. Uniting in one vast country is a challenging idea. What made it possible is the promise of tolerance. Ideals like religious freedom ensured that people could worship according to their beliefs without being subject to persecution. Freedom of speech delivered the right to voice dissent—even against the government, something that could easily lead to a charge of treason and a public execution in other times or places.[7]

While these ideals still hold true, they're being tested. Politicians play on division and stoke fear in order to garner votes. People frequently lament the lack of civil discourse. For many Americans, this situation brings forth a sense of powerlessness. What change can we possibly effect, given that most of us are not members of Congress and have little power? We long for a way to bring hope to a hurting world, and to ease our own sense of fear about what the future may hold.

One answer may be as simple as hospitality and thoughtful conversation. In 2010, a project was piloted with the goal of bringing people together in living rooms across the country to talk about the issues that divide them. The project was called Living Room Conversations, and it has continued to build on its early success. What's interesting about this model is that there's no attempt to come to an agreement. Instead, participants just come together, sometimes over a meal or refreshments, and practice speaking and listening to one another as people, not as enemies. It's another way hospitality could change the world.

---

7. Amy Chua and Jed Rubenfeld, "The Threat of Tribalism," *The Atlantic*, October 2018, https://www.theatlantic.com/magazine/archive/2018/10/the-threat-of-tribalism/568342/.

TRY THIS: *Take a look at the Living Room Conversations website at livingroomconversations.org. Commit to hosting or attending a gathering of people with different viewpoints. If a local gathering isn't available, you can also find a virtual gathering on the Living Room Conversations website. Whenever you encounter people with beliefs different than your own, whether it's an intentional conversation or not, practice listening with love. Try a breath prayer, "This person is a child of God," if you find yourself losing sight of this essential truth.*

Welcoming What Comes: Hospitality for Parents

We were sitting at the dinner table one night when my husband mentioned an upcoming business trip to New York City.

"Maybe we can go with you," I said. "Isabel has always wanted to go to New York City." She had, in fact, mentioned this more than once.

"What?" My daughter's incredulity came out in a near screech. "I do NOT want to go to New York City. I hate cities. Why would I want to go to a really big one?"

Personally, I'd always been surprised by her interest in visiting New York, but now I was surprised by her distinct lack of interest. *What had happened?*

What had happened was what happens to every parent: kids change.

They often change with a rapidity that leaves us breathless. We've had this same discussion over her favorite foods ("but you love chicken alfredo!"), clothes, hairstyles, and friends.

It can leave a parent feeling like they're always behind. This is disconcerting considering that these little people are *our* little people. We're supposed to know them better than anyone else in the world, not be strangers to their hopes and dreams.

The desire to maintain connection is partly what leads us to launch into pointless and unwinnable arguments, like whether or not a child wants to go to New York City. As parents, the movement of time is accelerated as we watch our children change right under our noses.

It's no wonder that the most common phrase among parents is, "Time goes by so fast!" The child who was once a snuggly baby becomes a toddler whose whole sole motivation in life is to run away. The kindergartner who loved chicken tenders soon becomes a fifth grader trying out vegetarianism.

Raising a child is a constant stream of second guessing, always wondering who they'll be today. This is why parenting is the ultimate act of hospitality. For as long as we are parents, we are entrusted with the care of a stranger. These are the people we are meant to love and care for, yet they are also the people we are learning to let go of. Their very existence demands our love while simultaneously asking us to remember that we are merely the starting place on their journey.

We learn to love deeply and hold loosely.

In our solemn recognition of the enormity of this task, it's easy to fall into a pattern that is more critical than affirming. At home, it plays out in a thousand daily routines. Rather than "Thank you for doing the dishes," we say, "Next time, please do a better job wiping the table."

We're just as hard on ourselves. Every day I come home from work with a list of things I could have done better. "The sermon was okay, but I wish I'd said this instead." "The meeting was fine, but I should have organized the agenda differently." I fall into bed each night with a list of the things that could have been better, rather than appreciation for whatever gifts I brought to each interaction.

What an inhospitable way to live! I imagine the shock if someone were to show up at my door for dinner, their lovingly made dessert in hand, and I replied, "This cake is fine but I wish you would have made chocolate." Now imagine if we repeated that scene over and over again, every time a guest dared to join us for game night or a potluck. It's so absurd, it's laughable. Yet, that is how we treat ourselves and sometimes even how we treat those we live with.

The inner critic runs strong, and it's stronger under stress or uncertainty. Faced with the urgencies of the world, I want to unleash a barrage of things we should be doing—to help, or fix, or get ready. The anxiety we feel trickles down to our children, the very people we are trying to protect. I've talked to many middle schoolers who are already overwhelmed with the number of things they should do or should be in their lives. "Where is there any hope?" one asked recently.

In our eagerness to prepare our children for the future, we are shutting down the skills they will need most. Hope and creativity—even in the midst of challenge—are foundational attitudes of resilience. They don't need a to-do list of what it'll take to save the world. They need a way of living into whatever comes.

This is where the practice of hospitality can offer us some guidance. Hospitality isn't the frenzied housecleaning of someone desperately trying to prove they're worthy; it's the openhearted confidence of someone who knows that no matter what appears on the threshold, they can handle it. A life lived this way, with openness to the future and confidence in our ability to make changes, would be well-lived.

TRY THIS: *Practice creative problem solving with your child. Ask, "What would you do about this?" the next time you're facing a challenge. Teachers often use this technique to build community and ownership, but I've had good luck asking it as long as I keep the questions age-appropriate. It's refreshing for kids to be on the advice-giving end and encouraging for them to know that their thoughts are valued.*

Kids and Hospitality

Many years ago, part of my work was coaching and consulting with preschool teachers as part of an early intervention program.

Sometimes I would arrive for a visit with a teacher before the students were there for the day, and when I did, I got a behind-the-scenes peek at classroom life. The teacher and I would chat while they made their way around the classroom, setting up exploration stations and scraping up stubborn bits of clay left-over from the day before. With each item lovingly set out, the room began to take on its own expectant energy. It reminded me of the way expectant parents will fold and refold blankets, or wander by the soon-to-be nursery and just stand there a minute, getting ready.

From my position as watchful observer, I can say with certainty that kids appreciate these acts of hospitality. They know when a room has been made ready for them. What a blessing it must be for a child, who has very little power in the world and is always at the mercy of others, to find a space where they are truly free to be themselves.

While it's commonplace today for classrooms and homes to have child-sized furniture and encourage open-ended play among children, this idea was relatively unheard of until Maria Montessori popularized it in the early 1900s. We know now that kids learn better in environments where they have more independence. Schools differ in educational philosophy and the capacity to create student choice, but all curriculums incorporate this to some extent. Young elementary students have learning centers, middle grades may be given time to pursue "passion projects," high schoolers get to choose their electives.

At home, too, we learn the efficacy of giving kids choices. Parent educators teach us to handle those toddler years by giving as much independence as we can. We're taught to head off difficult situations by offering choices like, "It's time to leave the park. Would you like to wear your coat or carry it?"

These are ways of practicing hospitality. We are making room for our kids to be their own people. We're welcoming them as they grow more fully into the many ways God is already working in them. When we approach this with curiosity and love, rather than a sense that we need to shape them, we are doing our part to live into God's vision for each little person in our lives. What this means is that kids learn to live hospitably. Because they do not have to fight for every little bit of autonomy, they are more open to welcoming others. It's not an overnight process. Two-year-olds will struggle to share their toys or their favorite snacks. These basic acts of hospitality run counter to their critical developmental stage of self-differentiation. Yet, the more they experience a generous and loving world, the more they want to emulate that.

We can help our kids practice hospitality throughout their lives. Learning to help guests feel comfortable on playdates and sleepovers goes hand-in-hand with learning the radical hospitality that can welcome "the stranger" in all kinds of ways. We can help them develop empathy with questions like, "What helps you feel comfortable when you are staying somewhere overnight?"

I saw the effect of good modeling when our church hosted an overnight shelter for people experiencing homelessness. In preparation, I asked a group of elementary students, "What would help make our church more comfortable for sleeping?" They came up with all kinds of ideas. Some were doable immediately, some had to be set aside for more time and bigger budgets. What was apparent, though, was that kids were connecting their own experiences of being welcomed at church to the experience of making room for others. "I always like it when we have room to run around and play games," one kid said. "We should make sure that there's plenty of room for the beds and just hanging out." Another made the connection between the snacks we have during fellowship time after Sunday services and the muffins we were making for the shelter. Others hoped there would be someone there to greet the guests as they arrived. "It's my favorite part of church!" they said.

The experience of giving and receiving hospitality had come full circle. Without any lecturing about what it means to be a good Christian, or a Bible study on the hospitality commands, the kids picked up on the things that make for a welcoming experience. We just had to model it and then provide the opportunity for them to put it into action.

TRY THIS: *The next time you're having guests over, ask your kids what makes them feel welcome at someone else's home. Help them implement these ideas at your home.*

Hospitality, Mindfulness, and Overcoming Anxious Thinking

The practice of hospitality can also give us some insight into our inner world and the worries that intrude on our prayer and meditation practices. For many years, I've tried letting intrusive thoughts flow by like clouds on the wind like a meditation teacher once taught me, or watching them drift by like boats on a river like a therapist taught me. Unfortunately, it seems my clouds and boats are very good at circling back.

I was looking at one of those vintage paintings of Jesus knocking on the door when I realized, our thoughts can be like this image of Jesus. They get stuck, perpetually knocking on the door. What happens if we just open the door?

Wisdom from mindfulness practices reinforces the importance of welcoming difficult sensations. In meditation, we learn that rather than trying to push intrusive thoughts away, it's better to simply acknowledge them. We don't have to stop them before they get a foot in the door. We let them in and we see them for what they are. Only when we've accepted and recognized them do we gently begin to change them.

Thinking of our thoughts like a guest can help when we start worrying about the future. There's a visualization practice I've begun for welcoming uncomfortable thoughts or feelings. It's easier to understand when it's personalized, so here's one way I used it during the economic downturn of the COVID-

19 pandemic. I had, of course, already done the usual things we do when we're faced with financial uncertainties: I asked my husband multiple times if his job was secure, and then ran our budget through my head a few times to see where we'd cut expenses if I lost mine.

There's wisdom in being prepared, but once I'd accomplished that, I needed to let the worries go. I imagined a knock on the door from someone who desperately needs help. They'd lost their job, run out of their savings, their friends had turned on them, and their children were floundering under the stress. It's dark and cold and, in desperation, the person has come to me. I could, of course, ignore the knock, but pretty soon the timid knock would turn into a frantic pounding. Perhaps they'd even resort to ringing the doorbell again and again. I might succeed in keeping them out of the house, but I'd also find myself distracted, with my fear and irritation building.

I considered what it would be like to open the door and attempt to reassure them. "It's fine. God will provide. This will all work out in the end." Naturally, I would say these things while also barricading the door with my body. My words say it's fine; my body says, "Go away before you ruin my life, too!" It's not exactly hospitable.

Or, I could invite them in. Perhaps I could even make them a cup of tea and listen to their problems. "That is scary," I might say tenderly.

And then I realized something. My guest isn't just here to vent, or get help, they're here to warn me. They're worried for my well-being. So instead of kicking them out, I could just graciously say thank you and walk them to the door. Feeling loved and cared for, maybe they'd leave quietly and I could take some time to evaluate which of their concerns need my attention.

What a loving way to treat ourselves and our worries!

My exercise in imaginary hospitality is similar to practices of self-compassion and mindfulness. In those practices, we don't let our anxieties take up permanent residence in our homes, sharing their doomsday prophecies with everyone they meet. Nor do we block them at the door, desperately trying to ignore them as they get louder and louder. Instead, we let them in, hear them out, assure them we can handle it, and then help them on their journey.

TRY THIS: *Do your own visualization experiment. What do your anxious thoughts look like? What would happen if you welcomed them instead of ignoring them or controlling them?*

A Blessing for Welcoming

May the light of Christ you shine on others
shine back on you.
And in this endless loop of light,
may peace, love, and mercy brighten all the dark corners
of a world waiting to be renewed.

Questions for Group or Personal Reflection

1. When have you felt especially vulnerable? What could have someone done to help ease that discomfort for you?
2. When was the last time you went out of your comfort zone to show hospitality?
3. How does it shift your view of parenting to think of your children as guests? What does it mean to be hospitable to your family members?
4. What is the most world-changing act of hospitality you could do? What would it take to make it work?

References and Resources

Chua, Amy and Jed Rubenfeld. "The Threat of Tribalism." *The Atlantic*, October 2018. https://www.theatlantic.com/magazine/archive/2018/10/the-threat-of-tribalism/568342/.

Leohas, Sorche Nic. *Always Room for One More.* New York: Henry Holt and Company, 1965.

Strauch, Alexander. *The Hospitality Commands*, Kindle edition. Littleton, CO: Lewis and Roth, 1993.

Willets, Dustin and Brandon Clements. *The Simplest Way to Change the World: Biblical Hospitality as a Way of Life.* Chicago: Moody Publishers, 2017.

CHAPTER 7

Generosity
Choosing Abundance

It takes generosity to discover the whole through others. If you realize you are only a violin, you can open yourself up to the world by playing your role in the concert.

—JACQUES-YVES COUSTEAU

Discovering Generosity

It was a hot day at the Community Food Share warehouse, and the air conditioning struggled to keep up. There were nine of us, three adults and six kids, assigned the task of sorting apples. Seven hundred and four pounds of apples, to be exact. They were in a huge cardboard container, the type that grocery stores use to display watermelons and pumpkins. Our task was to bag the edible ones up for the food pantry shelves and put the rotten ones into a bin for pickup by a local farmer to be used for animal feed.

An hour in, our backs hurt from bending into the apple container, our fingers hurt from tying the netting we used to craft bags, and our hands were sticky from handling rotten apples. At the end of the two-hour shift, though, we happily examined the boxes of newly sorted apples. We felt especially proud when the volunteer coordinator reported that each hour of volunteer work allows the pantry to provide ninety meals. The kids quickly calculated that they each provided one hundred and eighty meals. When the coordinator asked for a few volunteers to stay a little longer to help with clean up, it was a race to see who could get to the mop and rags first.

This seems funny to adults. One parent remarked, "I wish they'd work this hard at home." It's true; kids will often happily volunteer for things that they'd balk at doing at home.

We grown-ups aren't immune to this same feeling of goodwill that inspires action in kids. Service projects are a staple of congregational life. I've helped with home building or storm clean-up projects that require long days in hot conditions, exactly the kind of chore I put off doing at home. Volunteer work feels different though—likely due to what's sometimes called "the giver's high," that warm feeling that comes from knowing you've done meaningful work.

In a 2017 study, adult volunteers overwhelmingly reported a sense of increased well-being from volunteering, including higher self-esteem and improved mood. Most also reported feeling physically healthier due to their volunteer work.[1] Research suggests that volunteering is good for kids, too. It's linked to better grades and reduced drug use, among other benefits.[2]

Volunteering increases a sense of connection, and relationships and social support are tied to both happiness and health.[3] Volunteerism can also give us a sense of purpose, which is important for happiness and meaning-making. Contributing

---

1. United Health Group, "UnitedHealthcare Study Finds Americans Who Volunteer Feel Healthier and Happier," Sept 14, 2017, https://www.united healthgroup.com/newsroom/2017/0914studydoinggoodisgoodforyou.html.

2. Phillip Moeller, "Why Helping Others Makes Us Happy: Pursuing Self-Interested Goals Drives Ongoing Community Engagement and Raises Self-Esteem," *U.S. News*, April 4, 2012, https://money.usnews.com/money/personal-finance/articles/2012/04/04/why-helping-others-makes-us-happy.

3. Harvard Medical School, "The Health Benefits of Strong Relationships," *Harvard Women's Health Watch*, December 2010, updated August 6, 2019, https://www.health.harvard.edu/newsletter_article/the-health-benefits-of-strong-relationships.

positively to an otherwise out-of-control situation increases our sense of control, which reduces anxiety.

What researchers can't explain is why acts of service or charity *in particular* achieve this. After all, people can find connection in other ways. They might find meaning in work, or through a hobby. They also gain a sense of control by becoming more self-focused, as we see in times of crisis.

In truth, most people do all of these things to a certain extent. But many people also volunteer or give financially in big and small ways, and those who do find that the volunteer act brings a greater sense of joy or fulfillment than the other possibilities.

Some things can't be explained completely by science, at least not yet. Theologically speaking, we have some insight. One way to understand our desire to be helpful is that it is the divine spark, or universal love, alive in all of us. We might call it the Imago Dei, or image of God, in which humanity is rooted. These words honor the mystery that we are somehow deeply connected to God and to each other. The Christ light within us longs to shine in the world.

TRY THIS: *Send a small gift to someone who needs cheering up. Enjoy the act of finding and sending something unexpected.*

Christian Generosity (and Avoiding Sanctimonious Giver Syndrome)

In my own quest to be more generous, I've worked hard to overcome what I call "sanctimonious giver syndrome." It'll sneak up on me sometimes, often when I feel like an act of generosity is being taken for granted. It's recognizable by the wrong kind of pride. Not the happy "I made a difference" pride that is a sign we're on the right track and encourages us to keep doing more, but the kind of pride that people attribute to the false self, or the ego. It's the "I'm better than the people I'm helping" pride.

This may be what Jesus was getting at when he pointed out the difference between the widow's donation and the bigger donations given by wealthier people (Mark 12:41–44, Luke 21:1–4). The widow gave only a little, while the wealthy people gave a great deal. Still, Jesus lifted up the widow's donation as being greater because she gave all she had. The wealthy people gave what they felt they could afford.

That's the ever-present temptation when it comes to giving. How many times have I willingly splurged for a family trip and then carefully calculated what I could afford when it came to giving to a charity? Or when the holiday food collection rolls around and I'd fill my cart with all the treats I love before grabbing a couple jars of baked beans to throw into the food drive containers on the way out of the store?

I was challenged to think differently about this when I met with a food drive coordinator one summer. We were talking about doing a food drive for a lunch-for-kids program and she said, "We encourage our donors to give the same thing they buy for their kids at home. It's not because the families who come here are picky; if you buy store brand at home, by all means bring that here. We just ask people to be mindful of it as a spiritual practice. It's a way of giving from our first fruits."

The passage she was referring to is this one: "When you enter the land that I am giving you and you reap its harvest, you shall bring the sheaf of the first fruits of your harvest to the priest" (Leviticus 23:10).

The first fruits are the most sought after, the much-looked-forward-to first strawberry of spring. When we give away that coveted first taste, we remember that the people we give to are just as important as we are. They, too, have dreams and hopes, likes and dislikes.

The truth is, for most of my donations I don't directly interact with the people I give to. My food donations are shipped off along with everyone else's, my money is combined with everyone else's money. No one really knows whether I bought organic, low-sugar, fresh pressed juice for home and inexpensive, artificially colored juice for donations. No one, that is, but me.

After that conversation, I started to make my donations more intentionally. I made a list of the ways I could better give from my "first fruits." A few of my ideas were:

- Increase the total amount of my donations as a percentage of my budget.

- Buy the same food to donate that I buy for myself.

- Plan my Christmas gift budget by putting the Angel Tree gift first, not last.

My list is more of an inspiration than a system. Still, it's been a helpful framework to have in mind.

With my daughter, I've put it in practice in similar ways. When we bought shampoo one day, I made sure to give the instruction, "Get an extra bottle of the same kind you use for our church donation bin." Likewise when we bought first aid supplies for hurricane relief kits, or other donation purchases that she's been involved in. We've also used "Save, Spend, Share" jars for her allowance. The idea is that when she gets money, it's designated right away for a longer-term planned purchase, immediate spending money, and donations. By themselves, these seem like small examples, but they're teachable moments and ways to ensure that we're giving thoughtfully.

Introducing this idea of "first fruits" leads to interesting discussions. I was shopping with a youth group for school supplies, using money they'd raised themselves, when they faced a buying dilemma. Was it better to buy a lot of store-brand supplies or fewer name-brand supplies? Should they focus on helping as many kids as possible or on making sure that the kids they did help knew that they were valued? In the end, they decided on store brand for most things and name brand for the things kids really pay attention to. "After the first few weeks, everybody loses their fancy pens and pencils anyway. That's not worth the extra money. But it's really fun to have a cool-looking pencil holder, so let's spend a little more for some fun ones." Their decision seemed like a good compromise thoughtfully made.

TRY THIS: *Talk about the idea of giving from your "first fruits" with your kids. Are there ways they think the family could do this better? If your kids get an allowance, see if there's a way to add a giving practice to it. Can they donate a percentage of their allowance to an organization of their choosing?*

Doing For and Doing With

There's another way "sanctimonious giver syndrome" sneaks in, and it happens when we see ourselves as "more than" the people we're helping. We might think we're more capable, more invested in the outcome, or even more blessed than the people we're giving to. In those cases, our generosity comes from a sense of superiority.

An important corrective to this is when we learn to see ourselves in solidarity with others. We shift our thinking from "doing for" someone else to "working with" others. This difference is often talked about in terms of charity versus solidarity.

I was in a class for early interventionists when the trainer showed a picture of a parent reading a book on the couch. The living room around her was littered with toys. A mug sat on the coffee table in front of her, with some leftover bits of toast. A child's sippy cup was near that. On the other side of the room, a baby sat in a playpen.

"What do you see in this picture?" the trainer asked.

One by one, the group began naming things. The mom wasn't interacting with her baby. The room was a mess. There were leftovers sitting on the table. "Interesting," the trainer said, with the practiced voice of someone who's done this same exercise with many other groups of well-meaning educators and social workers. She went on to remind us that our work was "strengths-based," meaning our job was to look for the things that were going right in a situation and build on those. "Now what do you see?" she asked.

This time we noticed new things. The mom was reading a book. There was food for both her and the child on the table: everyone was being fed. The baby was happy in the playpen, not crying or distressed. There were plenty of toys.

This was a valuable reminder in itself. The real epiphany came when a young mom in the group spoke up. "I feel relieved hearing this looked at differently. I felt so judged the first time around. My house could look like the one in this picture at any given moment. Maybe the mom just needed a break and decided to read instead of cleaning. Maybe her house always looks like this because she's going to school or working, and cleaning is low-priority. Or maybe she really is struggling right now and she's reading a parenting book, trying to do better."

This is a perfect illustration of the oh-so-human assumptions we can make when we're trying to help someone. We assume that if they need help, it's because they've done something wrong. They don't have enough to eat because they don't manage their money well. They're homeless because they don't want to work. They're sick because they didn't take care of themselves. We confuse "helping" with "fixing."

In a charity mindset, we're doing *for* someone. In a solidarity mindset, we're working *with* them. We recognize that they know more about their life than we do. We also recognize that the problems are bigger than we'd like them to be.

While generosity benefits the giver, it's important that this benefit doesn't come at the expense of someone else's dignity. We can feel proud of the work we do, and we can get a sense of accomplishment from making a difference, but we can also be careful that the "giver's high" isn't an ego trip.

We can help kids develop a sense of solidarity by combining charitable giving with activism, as we'll see in the next section on project-based giving. We can also put relationships at the center of our generosity. When we get to know people, we better understand the complexities of the situation and we're more willing to listen to their wisdom about what needs to change. Several congregations I've served have had ministries for feeding or sheltering people who are experiencing homelessness. Every time, volunteers talk about how they were transformed by talking to the people they'd served. They relayed stories of people who had lost jobs through no fault of their own and wound up homeless, or of medical bills that got out of control. Time and again they relayed the heartbreak of veterans whose trauma made it difficult for them to keep a job. "Why don't we take better care of our military personnel?" one person asked after a long conversation.

These experiences help us change our mindset from charity to solidarity. As adults, we can start there. Whatever understanding we gain will be passed down in the way we talk to our children about the complicated issues of justice and social change. It's harder to find places for kids to volunteer where they can meet the people they're helping. In the internet age, however, it's never been easier to get access to personal stories. Often, nonprofit organizations have these on their website in their "stories" or "testimonials" section. Children's books, Storycorps interviews, blogs, and vlogs are all places we can find personal accounts to go along with the work we're doing.

TRY THIS: *Read a story about food scarcity with your kids, and talk about why people sometimes need help getting food. Feeding America has several stories on their website: www.feedingamerica.org/hungrytohelp. From there, you can download their Family Action Plan, which has a story about a family facing food insecurity, information about hunger in the United States, and actions families and kids can take. If you prefer a picture book, look for Maddi's Fridge by Lois Brandt at your local library. Notice together how Maddi and Sofia help each other. You might ask* *your kids why Sofia didn't want Maddi to tell anyone about her empty refrigerator. Other questions you could ask are: Why do you think Sofia didn't have any food? What do you think the moms talked about when the kids went out to play?*

Giving Counters Despair

As schools and businesses closed during COVID-19, people in my community were quick to look for volunteer opportunities. It seems it wasn't an isolated occurrence. In the United Kingdom, a governmental call for volunteers led to half a million people signing up for the National Health Services "volunteer army" in the first twenty-four hours.[4] Even as people were losing jobs or facing fears about their own health, they were eager to find ways to help others. Curious, I asked a few church members what drove them to volunteer. Some said it helped them feel grounded in an otherwise uneasy time or gave them a sense of purpose when other social identities were falling apart.

Hearing these responses, and remembering how much my daughter enjoyed sorting apples the previous summer, I started looking for a volunteer opportunity for us to do together. With news story after news story highlighting the increased needs at shelters, food banks, and other human services groups, I knew there must also be a need for more volunteers.

There was, with a caveat. Most of the organizations I'd previously worked with had increased their age limit. Even the resource center our church partners with was only allowing kids age sixteen and over, a fact we discovered when several families

4. Stephanie Tierney and Kamal R Mahtani, "Volunteering During the COVID-19 Pandemic: What Are the Potential Benefits to People's Well-Being?" The Center for Evidence Based Medicine, Oxford University, April 23, 2020, https://www.cebm.net/covid-19/volunteering-during-the-covid-19-pandemic-what-are-the-potential-benefits-to-peoples-well-being/.

showed up eager to volunteer with their middle schoolers for a church-sponsored lunch. The middle schoolers were reduced to sitting in chairs and playing on their phones while the adults packed lunches in carefully measured six-foot stations. It was exactly the reverse of the apple sorting situation. Kids who might have been okay with a couple hours of extra screen time at home left depressed and dejected. "There's nothing you guys were doing that I couldn't do," one of them said. "Some of those people were over sixty-five and were in more danger than we were! Why not let us help? Everyone complains about kids being self-centered, but no one trusts us to do anything meaningful."

While I was sympathetic to the concerns for safety and understand the abundance of caution that's necessary when making decisions at an organizational level, I couldn't help but agree. Kids' abilities and motivations are often underestimated.

Seeing the dejected faces of kids who weren't allowed to help confirmed something I'd long suspected: service to others is an antidote for despair.

Theologically speaking, despair is hopelessness. Psychologists add a few more descriptors, including powerlessness, helplessness, and a sense that a person can't "create a satisfactory future for oneself."[5] When the world feels out of control, we face options for how we'll cope. Some turn to denial or anger or self-preservation as ways of exercising control. Or we can try to make the world a better place. The second option is not only the Christian one, it's the one that ultimately feels better.

Getting kids involved in acts of service, generosity, and change-making is crucial to their well-being as well as to co-creating a better world.

---

5. Stephen A. Diamond, "Clinical Despair: Science, Psychotherapy and Spirituality in the Treatment of Depression," *Psychology Today*, March 4, 2011, https://www.psychologytoday.com/us/blog/evil-deeds/201103/clinical-despair-science-psychotherapy-and-spirituality-in-the-treatment.

TRY THIS: *Ask your kids what helps them feel hopeful. See if there's a way to include more of it, whatever "it" is, in your lives together.*

Teaching Generosity

As soon as my daughter could hold a spoon, she tried to feed me, mimicking the caretaking behavior she'd received over the first eighteen months of her life. It would be logical to assume this behavior is motivated by the praise a child gets from her doting parents, but one study replicated this common experience in order to determine a baby's motivation for sharing. It turns out that babies will offer food to a researcher in the absence of praise and even when the researcher is a stranger.[6] Babies appear to have a stronger internal capacity for sharing and selflessness than was previously thought.

Toddlers and preschoolers continue growing in what we call "pro-social" behavior as their physical skills develop. They're eager to help around the house, sometimes to the chagrin of their parents who know that they could often get the job done faster without their little helper. What developmental experts teach us is that there's tremendous benefit to encouraging a child's help even when it's not yet very helpful. People learn by doing. If we want our elementary school child to be able to sweep up after dinner, we're going to have let our preschooler give it a try. If we want them to know how to cook a meal when they've moved out of the house, we're going to have to suffer through some burned pancakes when they're young. It seems reasonable to extrapolate that to acts of generosity, which is one reason I'm passionate about connecting kids with meaningful volunteer activities.

---

6. Jill Suttie, "Even Hungry Babies Want to Share," *Greater Good Magazine*, May 4, 2020, https://greatergood.berkeley.edu/article/item/even_hungry_babies_want_to_share.

Researchers tell us that that generosity is connected to empathy. While teaching empathy might seem like a daunting task, we can teach it the same way I "taught" my daughter to share her food with me: by modeling. If you want to raise generous kids, then chances are you're generous yourself or you want to become more generous, or even more likely, you're both. Living your life in a generous way is the first step in teaching your kids to be generous. Plus, it goes both ways. Empathetic people are more generous, but people who have seen the difference that generosity makes are more empathetic.

Ideally, kids can participate in projects where they can see the effects of their work firsthand. The younger the child is, though, the harder these experiences are to come by. It takes work on the part of the adult. I've run a service learning group for kids for many years, and believe me, I know how inefficient it is if the only goal being measured is output. Over the years I've figured out a few projects that I've found work really well when age, location, or ability is a challenge to finding in-person volunteer opportunities:

- Make pet toys for an animal shelter.

- Make blankets for a safe house or homeless shelter.

- Check with your local soup kitchen to see if you can make cookies for them to use for a lunch. This used to be more common, but food safety rules have shifted and it's not allowed as much anymore. Still, it's worth a phone call.

- Make cards for people in assisted-living facilities.

- Do a neighborhood collection of food for your local food pantry. Some food pantries even have sample flyers and reusable bags you can pass out to people when you invite them to donate. If yours doesn't, it's pretty easy to find a sample online. What I like about this project is that you could do it every month.

Don't forget the personal things. So often we focus on volunteering with organizations, but see if there's someone in your church, apartment building, or neighborhood who could benefit from some help. Can your child offer to mow a lawn, pick up groceries, or make a meal for someone? Keep an eye out on social media pages. Some of my best projects for kids have come from there, but I had to get a little creative. Last year someone posted that they were collecting leftover Halloween candy to give away in Christmas stockings. I asked if our group could help sort the candy, which was a great project for the youngest kids and a tremendous help to the organization, which was inundated with candy.

These projects are all good ways to build a culture of generosity in your family, even if you can't volunteer onsite somewhere. (For a list with links to resources for these projects, visit my blog at ameliadress.com/service-projects or check out the many resources on the website Doing Good Together.)

TRY THIS: *Tell your kids about a time they were generous and how it inspired you.*

A Project-Based Approach to Generosity

There's a parable that's often told about the work of activism. In it, some people discover a baby floating in a stream. They rush to help, only to find that soon there's another baby floating in the stream. Every time they rescue one baby, more and more babies are found. Eventually, someone realizes that rescuing the babies isn't effective; someone needs to go upstream and see who keeps throwing babies in the water.

The urgent point of this fable hits home. Charity can only accomplish so much. Clearly we need a balance between charity and change-making. In the Bible, this need for long-term change is talked about in terms of justice:

Give justice to the weak and the orphan; maintain the right of the lowly and the destitute. (Psalm 82:3)

Or:

". . . learn to do good; seek justice, rescue the oppressed, defend the orphan, plead for the widow." (Isaiah 1:17)

In both of these examples, which are two of many from the Old and New Testaments, the emphasis is on fixing the problem itself. Psalm 82 notes that we must "maintain the right" of people in need, while Isaiah frames it in terms of correcting oppression. In Christianity, we sometimes talk about our vision for "the kingdom of God," a world that will be just and loving for all. More generally, this type of change-making work is referred to as activism or advocacy.

In recent years, we've seen a resurgence of youth-led activist movements, the biggest outpouring since teenagers rallied around anti-war causes in the 1960s.[7] Like young people then, kids today are looking for a way forward in a time of existential threat. Yet, despite the rise in youth-led movements, parents and other caring adults are often reluctant to talk about the challenges that kids are facing and the real changes that need to be made. Sometimes it's because we don't want to overload our children or add to their worry. Other times, it's because we don't want to push our personal passions on them. A mom recently told me that her daughter wanted to wear a Human Rights Campaign t-shirt to school and she hesitated, not wanting her child to "feel burdened" by her mom's activism.

What we see, though, is that many kids are not only capable of engaging in this kind of work, they're eager for it. They're also

---

7. Zachary Jason, "Student Activism 2.0: A look back at the history of student activism and whether today's protesters are making a difference." Ed: Harvard Ed Magazine. Fall 2018. https://www.gse.harvard.edu/news/ed/18/08/student-activism-20.

eager to connect it to their faith. I think this is because they're well-attuned to anything that feels like a brush-off or false hope. For that reason, it's important to encourage and support kids in advocacy work in addition to the more common "service projects." We need a way of thinking about generosity that spans the breadth of the work we're called to do. I call this "project-based generosity."

Like many families, our family has a budget. Housing, groceries, fun, childcare, transportation, clothes . . . we have the usual list of expenses. Because generosity is a value we share, my husband and I have a line item for donations as well. That part we agree on. What we've struggled with, both individually and as a couple, is *where* to give. There are so many worthy causes. For many years, our giving was dictated largely by who asked. The church was raising money for hurricane victims: there went some of our money. A flyer from Doctors Without Borders arrived in the mail—there went a few dollars. We'd weigh the need of each cause as it came up, checking in to see where we were with our budget.

This is how many families allot their charitable donations. They give where they can, when the need arises. The same is true of volunteer opportunities. A few hours go to running the PTA book sale at the kids' school this month, next month it's volunteering at the church's rummage sale.

There is nothing wrong with budgeting time and money this way. It's part of our Christian calling to meet the needs of those around us as they arise. As the book of James (2:15–16) says, "If a brother or sister is naked and lacks daily food, and one of you says to them, 'Go in peace; keep warm and eat your fill', and yet you do not supply their bodily needs, what is the good of that?" On the other hand, we might benefit from adding some focus to our donations of time, money, and passion.

In her book *Simple Giving: Easy Ways to Give Every Day*, author Jennifer Iacovelli talks about several models for giving, ranging from everyday acts of kindness to the importance of giving as part of a business model. One of the most interesting ideas she explores is the idea of philanthropic giving.

Typically when we think of philanthropic giving, we think about big-name donors, like the people whose names appear on plaques at the local museum or on church pews. Iacovelli challenges this idea, saying that philanthropy is really about our emotional and personal investment in a cause or charitable organization. That can mean money or time or both, but the emphasis isn't on the act or donation itself. Instead, the emphasis is on our connection to the organization and our dedication to the work they do.[8] In this framework, philanthropic giving is about focus. Rather than giving a little bit of time here and a little bit of money there, we could give more of both to one organization or cause.

I'm reminded of a woman I knew through the world of early childhood education. A former preschool teacher herself, her face fairly shone with passion for the work. She donated money to a local nonprofit that worked on improving the quality of early education. She could always be counted on to show up at County Commissioner meetings if something that impacted young kids was on the agenda. She served on the board of directors for another preschool after she retired from teaching herself. She was dedicated to the work, and because of her dedication she inspired others.

When I think about the kind of giver I'd like to be, that's what comes to mind. Being someone whose dedication spills out, not just in the time and money they give, but in the way their passion becomes contagious. We become personally invested in the work we're supporting.

One way to live out a philanthropic mindset is to adopt a project-based approach to giving. Project-based learning is an educational strategy that focuses on helping kids design, research,

---

8. Jennifer Iacovelli, *Simple Giving: Easy Ways to Give Every Day* (New York: Jeremy P. Tarcher-Penguin, 2015).

and implement a project in order to deepen their knowledge and skills. Kids start with a question, then do in-depth research to explore the topic, and finally prepare some type of project that addresses the initial question.

What makes this different from a traditional research paper or book report is that there's both depth and choice built into the process. Students have choice in the topic itself, how they'll research it, and how they'll present it. There's exploration and hands-on learning throughout. There's also room for experimentation, failure, and success.

In schools, the advantage of project-based learning is that it builds a bridge between skills and content areas. Rather than having a child learn about the rainforest, then learn math, then do a unit on writing, teachers help kids design projects in which students are using their math and writing skills in order to learn about the rainforest. Kids can also tailor it to connect to something they're interested in, which helps their motivation and retention.

In project-based giving, we take the strengths of the project-based learning model and apply it to our family giving and volunteering. That means that we:

1. Tap into the interests of kids and adults in the family
2. Include deeper learning into the area
3. Combine financial giving, volunteer effort, and advocacy or activism

My daughter's passion is animals. She's donated her birthday money to the local animal shelter, and she's eagerly awaiting the day when she can volunteer there. Until then, we've done some projects at home like making blankets or toys for animals in shelters. This is a good start. Rather than simply liking animals, my daughter has learned to take the next step and look for ways to care for those animals who are in need of homes. With a little more intentionality on our part, we could deepen this learning by partnering with her to research an issue of animal welfare and then take steps toward making a change. She might discover an animal welfare law in our state that she'd like to see changed and then write a letter to a state representative.

This approach can also help address the false dichotomy between charity and changemaking. Often, people talk about these two ways of serving as though they're opposites. People who value the work of justice and systemic change point out that charity is a "band-aid" solution. It doesn't get to the root of the problem.

People who are drawn to the work of caring for individuals in their time of need point out that activism and long-term engagement overlook the immediate needs. However, it's an unfortunate and persistent truth that both are needed in our world. "Since there will never cease to be some in need on the earth, I therefore command you, 'Open your hand to the poor and needy neighbor in your land,'" as Deuteronomy 15:11 says.

Some people may be more readily suited to the work of advocacy while others are better suited to the work of individual care and healing, but at some level we're all called to both. Envisioning our work as philanthropic, or project based, helps us see the possibilities for deeper engagement, and by doing so we can embody hope in a hurting world.

TRY THIS: *Individually or with your family, think of a cause that's important to you. Can you think of a few ways to invest in it that combine generosity on multiple levels: service, donations, and advocacy?*

A Blessing for Abundance

For stretching to give beyond what feels comfortable,
For choosing hope in times of fear,
For living abundance when others create scarcity,
May you be blessed.

Questions for Group or Personal Reflection

1. Martin Luther once said that our hands have fingers so that things can slip through them. In other words, we were made to give. Do you agree? To what extent do you think generosity is inherent or taught?

2. What comes most naturally to you: service/volunteering with a charity, donating money, or advocacy work? How could you become more "project based" in your generosity?

3. How have you given from your "first fruits"? What other ways have you found to avoid "sanctimonious giver syndrome"?

4. Were you more or less interested in justice issues when you were a teenager? If you changed either direction, why do you think that is? What support could you offer to the youth-led movements of today?

References and Resources

Diamond, Stephen A. "Clinical Despair: Science, Psychotherapy and Spirituality in the Treatment of Depression." *Psychology Today*, March 4, 2011. https://www.psychologytoday.com/us/blog/evil-deeds/201103/clinical-despair-science-psychotherapy-and-spirituality-in-the-treatment.

Iacovelli, Jennifer. *Simple Giving: Easy Ways to Give Every Day.* New York: Jeremy P. Tarcher-Penguin, 2015.

Harvard Medical School. "The Health Benefits of Strong Relationships." *Harvard Women's Health Watch*, published December 2010, updated August 6, 2019. https://www.health.harvard.edu/newsletter_article/the-health-benefits-of-strong-relationships.

Lufkin, Bryan. "Coronavirus: The Psychology of Panic Buying." BBC Worklife, March 4, 2020. https://www.bbc.com/worklife/article/20200304-coronavirus-covid-19-update-why-people-are-stockpiling.

Moeller, Phillip. "Why Helping Others Makes Us Happy: Pursuing Self-Interested Goals Drives Ongoing Community Engagement and Raises Self-Esteem." U.S. News, April 4, 2012. https://money.usnews.com/money/personal-finance/articles/2012/04/04/why-helping-others-makes-us-happy.

Suttie, Jill. "Even Hungry Babies Want to Share." *Greater Good Magazine*, May 4, 2020. https://greatergood.berkeley.edu/article/item/even_hungry_babies_want_to_share.

Tierney, Stephanie and Kamal R Mahtani. "Volunteering During the COVID-19 Pandemic: What Are the Potential Benefits to People's Well-Being?" The Center for Evidence Based Medicine, Oxford University, April 23, 2020. https://www.cebm.net/covid-19/volunteering-during-the-covid-19-pandemic-what-are-the-potential-benefits-to-peoples-well-being/.

United Health Group. "UnitedHealthcare Study Finds Americans Who Volunteer Feel Healthier and Happier." September 14, 2017. https://www.unitedhealthgroup.com/newsroom/2017/0914studydoinggoodisgoodforyou.html.

CHAPTER 8
Silence
Experiencing Peace

True silence is the rest of the mind; and is to the spirit, what sleep is to the body, nourishment and refreshment.
—WILLIAM PENN

Discovering Silence

My own fascination with silence began during a busy and loud time in my life. We'd had extended family living with us off and on for quite a while, our house was stretched to the limit by extra adults, kids, and pets. At work, I spent most of my time talking to people, often visiting classrooms full of wonderful, loud children. My office was a shared cubicle. I was surrounded by noise.

It didn't take very long before I felt a pressure building up deep inside me. I stopped sleeping, and no amount of intense exercise or high-dose sleeping pills could lull me to peace. It was as though someone was turning a lever, like a wind-up car about to be set free. I began daydreaming about taking a vacation, not to some exotic beach but to a silent retreat center. I wasn't just looking for silence in my ears but silence in my soul. The external noise had shaken me internally.

This experience is one reason I've come to incorporate more opportunities for silence in church for people of all ages. One of our Sunday morning routines in a multi-age children's class is to spend one minute (yes, a full sixty seconds) in silence. Despite what I know about the importance of silence, it still terrifies me. Shouldn't I be doing something more with this time? Something to ensure engagement and happiness? It would save me some anguish to fill this time with a silly game and a lot of laughter. And sure, there are some Sundays when kids are more fidgety, but for the most part, they love this time.

Yes, you read that right. The kids love sitting in silence. Every Sunday, I am reminded that in our noise-filled, active lives, even these little bundles of energy need times of intentional quiet. This is how I set it up:

> God talks to us in a lot of different ways. Sometimes God talks to us through our friends, sometimes in nature, sometimes in music, sometimes through the stories of the Bible. But sometimes God also talks to us very quietly, right inside our hearts. So here we practice listening to God by spending some time in silence. This is what will happen. You'll feel wiggly at first. Then your body and your mind will settle down, and you'll start feeling more peaceful. To help your mind settle down faster, you can try focusing on the candle. Or you can repeat a word to yourself that helps you think of God, like "Jesus," "Peace," "Spirit," or "Christ." Or you can quietly count your breath. We'll be quiet together for sixty seconds. I'll keep track of the time so you don't have to. Let's all take a deep breath together and then we'll be silent.

After our time of quiet, I ask the kids how it went for them, and sometimes the kids report it was hard to settle down or they were distracted by noise in the hall, but nearly always some child will respond, "It was amazing."

The children are responding to the same inner longing I had experienced. Silence is increasingly rare. And I'm not the only one who finds that this provokes real, physical, mental, and spiritual anxiety.

Here's the correlation: In noisy environments, our cortisol levels rise.[1] Increased cortisol leads to higher blood pressure, which may lead to heart disease and risk of stroke. This increased cortisol also floods our brains with stress messages. Over time, these constant stress messages actually change the way our brains work, resulting in an effect similar to the response people have after long-term exposure to trauma or even PTSD.

That's just the effect of the noise itself, like the persistent sounds of busy environments. We also face challenges due to certain sources of noise. Persistent exposure to news increases our feelings of stress—repeated exposure can even lead to a trauma response. In a surprising study, researchers found that repeated exposure to media about the Boston Marathon bombing was associated with higher levels of trauma than witnessing the attack itself.[2] It's not just news. Social media, for all of its power to connect individuals, has been linked to increased anxiety and lower self-esteem.[3]

Clearly, silence is a something we need.

TRY THIS: *Keep track of the noises around you for one day. How much of your day is filled with noise? Where do you find time for quiet?*

Silence and Spiritual Renewal

This noisy world also affects our spiritual health. Too much noise makes it hard for us to hear the internal voice of our soul. This is

1. Amy Novotney, "Silence, Please," *Monitor On Psychology* 42 (2011): 46, accessed June 10, 2018, http://www.apa.org/monitor/2011/07-08/silence.aspx.

2. Alison E. Holman, Dana Rose Garfin, and Roxane Cohen Silver, "Media's Role in Broadcasting Acute Stress Following the Boston Marathon Bombings," PNAS, National Academy of Sciences, January 7, 2014, https://www.pnas.org/content/111/1/93.abstract.

3. Rebecca Granet, "Social Media's Effects on American Teens," CBS New York, September 19, 2016, https://newyork.cbslocal.com/2016/09/19/social-media-use-teens/.

why religious traditions stress the importance of silence. In Jewish and Christian traditions, we draw on the story of Elijah, who finds that God isn't present in noise and action, but in the quiet:

> Now there was a great wind, so strong that it was splitting mountains and breaking rocks in pieces before the Lord, but the Lord was not in the wind; and after the wind an earthquake, but the Lord was not in the earthquake; and after the earthquake a fire, but the Lord was not in the fire; and after the fire a sound of sheer silence. When Elijah heard it, he wrapped his face in his mantle and went out and stood at the entrance of the cave. Then there came a voice to him that said, "What are you doing here, Elijah?" (1 Kings 19:11–13)

Elijah found God in the stillness, not the dramatic acts of power that preceded it.

It is especially telling that this story comes in the midst of danger and deep fear for Elijah. He has fled for his life from King Ahab, running until the fear completely overtakes him. When he stops, he prays for death. In modern language, we would describe this as an episode of depression and anxiety. After fighting so hard and so long to show the righteousness of God, Elijah is overcome with hopelessness. I imagine he is facing the questions we all face in moments of existential threat. There, under the broom tree, Elijah wonders if any of this really matters. The things he's done that seemed so important at the time now seem empty.

There is no immediate resolve to Elijah's angst. An angel comes, but not to kill Ahab and Jezebel and therefore keep Elijah safe. Instead, the angel gives Elijah the most practical care when life feels overwhelming: a snack, a drink of water, and a good night's sleep. After these things, Elijah finds the strength to travel another forty days, where he once again cries out to God and is rewarded by finding God in the silence, experiencing a new clarity of purpose.

The Bible has plenty of stories that illustrate God's presence in flashes of light and bursts of noise; in fact, there are times when God's presence *is* found in earthquakes and fires. Moses sees God as a burning bush; there are "tongues like fire" on the day of Pentecost, when the Holy Spirit descends on the crowd of Jesus's followers. Elijah's story isn't telling us God is *never* present in noise, but that God is *also* present in silence. It provides a corrective of sorts. Otherwise, we would always be looking for God in the flashiness of life and missing out on the holiness that happens in subtle, profound ways.

TRY THIS: *Sit in the silence of nature, even if it's near a small plant in your home. Do you experience God's presence differently in that space? Consider creating a dedicated prayer or meditation area and incorporating items from the natural world in it.*

Pause and Think

A curious word appears in the Old Testament, mainly in the psalms. In Hebrew, it looks like this:

הֶלָס

We don't quite know what to do with this word. It has lost its meaning over the centuries and it has no English translation. We simply transliterate it, replacing its Hebrew letters with English ones and pronouncing it "selah." This is how it looks in Psalm 3 in the New Revised Standard Version:

> O Lord, how many are my foes!
>   Many are rising against me;
> many are saying to me,
>   "There is no help for you in God."
>   *Selah*
> I cry aloud to the Lord,
>   and he answers me from his holy hill.
>   *Selah*

Three times, total, the psalm repeats this word "selah." Commentators offer several ideas as to what selah might indicate. It may have meant something like "amen," as a sign of agreement or sympathy with the words. Since the psalms have often been sung or chanted, it may be a notation that indicates a musical interlude. Some scholars think selah indicates a pause of some kind, something like a punctuation note to the reader. We could compare it to a rest note in music, "When you perform this, take a rest here." If this is the case, selah would invite us to give emphasis to the words through a moment of quiet. Today, when we have ready access to our own Bibles to read and study on our own, we would do well to take that punctuation mark as an instruction for ourselves as well as a "performance note." For this reason, I like the Amplified Bible's translation of selah as "pause, and calmly think of that."

> Salvation belongs to the Lord; may your blessing be on your people! (Pause, and calmly think of that.) (Psalm 3:8, Amplified Bible, Classic Edition)

The very fact that the author of the psalms felt the need to indicate a pause tells us something about our human tendencies to go too quickly and too loudly. One of the first things children do when they learn to read is show off their speed. "Listen to how fast I can read this!" Then they rush through, crashing their way toward a triumphant ending: "Ta-da!"

Parents and teachers sit through these endless readings, appreciating the child's passion for a newly learned skill, all the while knowing the story would actually be better if it was slowed down. In rushing to get through the words of the book, the story itself has been lost. We find in these "selah" marks a reminder to slow down, linger over the words, and listen more intently for one brief moment.

It would be nice if all of life's great moments came with an indication of when we ought to pause. "Life is chaotic and hard right now, pause and catch your breath." "This is a beautiful, joyous moment, so pause and let it fill your soul."

Not having these cues, we find it hard to pause and listen. This is especially true when we are experiencing a sense of anxiety or pressure. In moments of crisis, real or perceived, our instinct is to rush. Our thoughts whirl, our hearts race. It seems like we need to do more: faster and louder than before.

Selah. Selah reminds us that this isn't true. In its mystery we are reminded of a truth we all hold deep inside. God is just as likely to be found in the quiet times as in the momentous occasions of our lives. Pause, and calmly think of that.

Who's Afraid of a Little Quiet?

It took over a year to get my silent retreat. When I crested the corner and saw the retreat center ahead, I sighed a deep sigh. Here I was, finally.

The hostess showed me around the facility, gave me instructions for lunch, and left me in a pleasant but sparse room. No TV, no radio, no cellphone. Wandering outside, I found myself staring at a marble bench. "Be still and know" was carved into the side. Much to my surprise, it seemed mocking in the cool spring air. Here I was, being still. What, exactly, was I supposed to know? Where was the big revelation I was supposed to find in all this quiet?

One of the interesting effects of overstimulation, whether it's noise, video games, food, or drinks, is that it feeds on itself. Stimulation leads us to want more stimulation. This is why overtired children start jumping on the couch or refusing to go to bed, or why a sugary breakfast causes us to crave sugar the rest of the day. It's why we keep tuning into the news, or refreshing our feed, even when we know there's nothing new to hear.

In that moment, my resistance to embracing the silence reminded me of something else. It felt a bit like my childhood fear of the dark. My siblings and I would rush from room to room, quickly flipping on lights, intent on illuminating the dark corners before any bogeymen could jump out and get us. Was I afraid of the quiet?

Later I wondered why so many of us find it so impossible to simply be within ourselves, without the constant noise of the outside world. What is the risk we are afraid to take? Unlike the darkness, which we banish because we are afraid of what's in it, perhaps we banish the silence because we're afraid of what *isn't* in it.

It is one thing to read the words of wise teachers who promote the benefits of time spent quietly. It is another to risk this exchange ourselves. What if we set aside time to commune with God or our deeper selves and find they are missing? What if, on that cold marble bench, I discovered that my stillness brought only emptiness—that there was nothing new to know?

Silence is a tremendous act of faith. Each time we dare to enter into the unknown quiet of our minds, we risk a great deal. We risk discovering something we do not like, something that doesn't fit with who we thought we were. Maybe if left alone to our inner thoughts, we learn there's nothing particularly deep there. As Anthony Strano says in *Seeking Silence,* noise becomes a way of "living superficially and haphazardly" to avoid "the unsettling reality of personal emptiness."[4]

One of the many lessons that came out of the early stay-at-home orders of the COVID-19 pandemic is that it's hard to sit with our emptiness. Streamed entertainment rose by nearly one hundred percent for people ages twenty-five to fifty-four as they sought to fill their time.[5] I heard from others who hoped they'd

4. Anthony Stanos, *Seeking Silence: Exploring and Practicing the Spirituality of Silence* (New York: Sterling Ethos, 2011), 6.

5. Tina Pukonen, "4 Entertainment Trends Marketers Can Leverage to Boost Spirits—and Revenues," Pinterest Business blog, May 19, 2020, https://business.pinterest.com/en/blog/4-entertainment-trends-marketers-can-leverage-to-boost-spirits-and-revenue.

use this time to meditate or pray or simply sit more, and instead struggled with the loneliness of that endeavor. A time of crisis is not the best time to learn a new skill, so there's no judgment as I point out the difficulties people faced or admit to my own increased movie-watching.

What this shows us is the importance of building these skills before we need them. We do ourselves a great favor when we make time to pursue quiet because we will face a time in our lives when quiet is thrust upon us. In those moments, we'll be glad we know how to experience stillness and listen for God. As one person said, drawing on their own background as a Quaker where silence is the central community practice, "There is a kindness in giving ourselves silence. This time alone has not been easy, and I've had to relearn what I know about finding God in quiet. But I'm grateful to be relearning it, rather than learning it fresh."

TRY THIS: *Practice unplugged mornings to cultivate inner peace as well as outer silence. Don't reach for your phone right away after waking up. Instead, give yourself half an hour of tech-free time to connect with what's really important.*

Silence for Parents

If making time for silence seems daunting, I'd offer the encouragement that silence doesn't have to be a Big Event. Despite the fact that a silent retreat proved to be a pivotal moment for me, I stand firm in the idea that perfection is the enemy of the good. During that same noisy time in my life, a therapist advised me to meditate twenty minutes a day, claiming that anything less than that was ineffective. While she was helpful in a thousand other ways, the mandate to find twenty minutes to sit in stillness had exactly the opposite effect. Faced with the hopelessness of finding twenty minutes alone and the wastefulness of doing anything less, I didn't even try five minutes. Instead, I continued careening around in a constant state of noisy pressure. This changed one Lent when I decided to take on the practice of contemplative prayer every day. This prayer practice requires a great deal of time spent in silence, quieting the mind and learning to listen for God. I was craving it, but I struggled with it. As I talked to my spiritual director about it later, she was encouraging. "What was it that you hoped to achieve with this practice?" she asked. With her thoughtful question, I realized that I just needed some quiet in my life. "Maybe it's not the practice itself," she said. "Maybe it's the lofty goals you're setting around it." With that in mind, she suggested smaller goals like turning the radio off when I'm in the car alone or doing my housework without a podcast in my ear.

Although her suggestions were substantially less "holy" in my mind, they were also much more attainable. And, as I became more practiced in having quiet around me during my daily routines, it became easier to build to a practice of sitting in intentional silence. Soon, I was able to sit in longer periods of quiet and prayer.

In order to achieve the revolutionary possibilities of quiet, we first have to train ourselves and our bodies to experience silence. When I say "experience silence," I don't mean suffer through it, agitated and fidgety, the way we might experience a boring meeting, but to experience the depths of silence. That means pressing through the initial discomfort that comes when we take on a quiet practice—a "detox" phase, if you will. With kids, it also means building slowly and having patience.

One aid to learning silence is to practice it as a group. Sometimes, brief silent prayer in church, a meditation class, or even family prayer feels more fulfilling and easier to manage than keeping a practice of individual silence. That's probably because a little peer pressure is a helpful thing. It's also true that we experience a different quality to the energy when we're quiet in the presence of another human being.

Sitting in silence with another is an intimate experience. We've all known those "awkward silences" after someone tells a bad joke or asks a silly question, but usually group silence is marked by acceptance and love. Think of the way a new couple walks hand-in-hand on the beach in quiet, the comfortable companionship of two friends just happy to sip coffee together without speaking, or even the slightly exhausted silence of a yoga class practicing *Shavasana*.

One Sunday away from my regular congregation and all the Sunday morning duties, I decided to explore this further by attending a Friends Meeting. Friends, or Quakers, structure their worship services almost entirely in silence. I'd been wanting to attend one for years, but struggled to find one at a time and location I could make it. Thanks to the wonders of technology and the forced move of services to an online format during the pandemic, I was able to attend a virtual service.

"I suspect this won't be the same experience as it would be in person," I wrote to a friend in an email just before the service began. I fully anticipated that sitting in silence while staring at my laptop would be boring and unengaging. Instead, the silence settled on me easily and with a sense of welcome. Despite our distance, it seems as though we were all connected in that quiet. I finally understood why Friends describe silence as "sacramental," meaning that it's a way Christ is made known.

TRY THIS: *Like monastic traditions that pray at certain times of the day, we can create brief rituals of quiet. Set an alarm for 8:00 a.m., noon, 4:00 p.m., and 8:00 p.m., and commit to being quiet for one minute at each of those times. Consider using a chime or gentle song tone instead of a buzzer. Or, go the reverse route by setting "noisy times" in your house. Between the hours of 9:00 a.m. and 6:00 p.m., for example, noise is fair game. Outside of* *those hours, TVs, phones, and radios are turned off or can only be used with earbuds.*

Kids and Silence

While teaching people to sit in silence sounds pretty tame, I'm convinced that it's actually revolutionary. The truth is that silence often isn't promoted by religion, or by government, by our jobs, or by any group of people that depends on "higher-ups" to make decisions.

When we encourage people to make time for silence, we remind them that there's a higher authority than whatever leadership is in effect. When I teach kids at church to make time for silence, I'm letting them know that they have direct access to God, anytime, anywhere, and I'm showing them one way to get there. I'm cutting out the middleman. It's inherently risky. It means that they might have different experiences of God than I have; it means they might come to different understandings about God than I do. It means that they may learn to trust their internal compasses, or find God calling them to something new.

The truth is that a great many people don't want to *learn* silence. Silence is hard. It's hard to turn off the radio with the upbeat music and disconnect from the happy feeling we get from singing along in order to sit quietly. It's hard to sit in church for a couple minutes and just *be*, rather than sitting in church and listening to a sermon or singing a song.

When we make time for silence, we're accepting a tremendous challenge as well as a tremendous responsibility. We're building in time to wrestle with God, and when we dare to make time to hear God's voice, we never know where that call will lead us.

This is why I believe the practice of keeping silence is so crucial for children. It serves two purposes:

1. A quietude practice gives them space to hear God's voice. This is crucial for a lifelong journey of faith.
2. Teaching kids to practice silence also teaches them that we value their intrinsic spirituality and human dignity. Time to listen to one's own thoughts and be open to God's presence is distinctly anti-authoritarian. It tells a child, "You have as much access to God as I do. Your thoughts are as worthy of attention as mine are."

I know it can be difficult to convince children to sit in silence. Until we've experienced it, we don't know what we're missing. Start small. Take a quiet walk as a family, or turn off the radio when you're in the car. Share your own silence practice to model its importance. When you invite kids to sit in silence, consider giving them something to fidget with. Say something like, "Let's just take a few moments to see what God is saying to us. Want to sit next to me and doodle while we listen for God's voice?" Afterwards, ask them if they heard or felt anything they'd like to share. This question is important for reinforcing to the child that they matter, and that you believe and care for their spiritual voice. Here are some things kids have told me they've experienced in a quiet time:

> I saw myself as lost in woods, and then God provided water and sharp things to hunt with.

> I saw a hawk circling above me, and it was saying, "I am with you."

> I didn't hear any words, but I imagined the clouds like angels watching over me.

These comments are from a group of second graders at a camp where I was chaplain. Some of them were part of congregations that had a practice of quiet, so they were familiar with the idea. Others had never sat in prayerful silence. All of them came to love our time of silence and sharing.

It's helpful to remind kids, "Sometimes it's hard to feel God. Sometimes I sit in silence and don't hear anything. That's okay." Or, "You don't have to share. I know some things are too special to share. Sometimes when I feel God, I don't know how to describe it." I also want to note that I have much better luck eliciting sharing in groups of kids than I do at home. Maybe that's because silence and reflection is easier in groups, or maybe it's just my daughter and her resistance to being pastored as well as "mommed" by me. Create silence and meaningful reflection where you can, but know that even when it's imperfect or it seems like kids aren't engaging, they're soaking up more than we think.

TRY THIS: *Do an active form of contemplation. Silence doesn't have to mean sitting. If you're a runner, try running without music. Others might take a quiet walk. Some people have found that keeping their hands busy helps with the antsy feeling. For them, activities like knitting or coloring are ways of prayerful silence.*

When God Is Silent

We have considered the many possibilities for increased happiness, better health, and deeper connection with God through times of silence. I firmly believe that people would do better with more time for quiet in our noisy, anxiety-producing world. However, it's dishonest to overlook the reverse possibility: sometimes it is God who is silent.

Saint Teresa of Calcutta, whom we know as Mother Teresa, wrestled deeply with this. In letters to her spiritual confidant published in 2007 in the book *Come Be My Light*, she lamented that God was absent from her. This was not a brief period of doubt or a flash of uncertainty. It was a longstanding spiritual struggle, one that persisted throughout her life. Unlike Elijah, who found God in the silence, Teresa again and again found only emptiness.

It is hard, as people of faith, to know what to make of these experiences. It is rare to find someone who has not experienced this, although for some it is short lived. We sometimes call these experiences "dark nights of the soul," after St. John of the Cross, who wrote about his own experiences of God's absence.

There are few things more painful. For those of us who find strength and courage in our faith, the experience of God's silence is soul crushing. While many people have experienced it, it defies pat explanation.

What we do know is that people often come out of it with a deepened sense of their relationship with God. For some, it becomes the turning point in a more mystical understanding of God's presence. For others, it seems to be connected with a conversion experience, or a shifting understanding of God. Whatever leads up to it, and whatever results from it, it's fair to say that it is painful. It's also fair to take what comfort we can from the knowledge that many others have walked this road. It may be less important to know why it happens as much as it is to allow something new to come from it. It is another way of living resurrection.

TRY THIS: *If you're beginning a practice of silent prayer or medi-tation, experiment with using a focus object to settle your mind. I like to focus on a lit candle. Other people find it helpful to use a piece of art or an item from nature. These can be ways of giving yourself something soothing to focus on so you're able to better tune out the sights and sounds around you.*

A Blessing for a Time of Quiet

As you step into the great unknown,
May the silence welcome you like a friend

Enfolding you in peace, holding you in love,
and sending you out in joy.

Questions for Group or Personal Reflection

1. People have varying capacities for noise tolerance. Do you have a higher or lower noise threshold? What noises make you feel irritable and distracted? What sounds bring you a sense of peace and calm?

2. When have you experienced God's presence, or something you might even describe as the voice of God? What helped open you up to that experience?

3. What do you think about the idea that silence requires faith?

4. If someone could label parts of your life "selah," to remind you to pause and think, what parts of the day do you most need that reminder?

5. Have you ever been part of a silent meditation, prayer practice, or observed a moment of silence with a group? How does it compare to experiences of meaningful silence while alone?

References and Resources

Bill, J. Brent. *Holy Silence: the Gift of Quaker Spirituality*, Kindle edition. Grand Rapids, MI: William B. Eerdmans, 2016.

Holman, E. Alison, Dana Rose Garfin, and Roxane Cohen Silver. "Media's Role in Broadcasting Acute Stress Following the Boston Marathon Bombings." PNAS, National Academy of Sciences, January 7, 2014. https://www.pnas.org/content/111/1/93.abstract.

Granet, Rebecca. "Social Media's Effects on American Teens." CBS New York, September 19, 2016. https://newyork.cbslocal.com/2016/09/19/social-media-use-teens/.

Pukonen, Tina. "4 Entertainment Trends Marketers Can Leverage to Boost Spirits—and Revenue." Pinterest Business blog, May 19, 2020. https://business.pinterest.com/en/blog/4-entertainment-trends-marketers-can-leverage-to-boost-spirits-and-revenue.

Stanos, Anthony. *Seeking Silence: Exploring and Practicing the Spirituality of Silence*. New York: Sterling Ethos, 2011.

CHAPTER 9

Blessing
Healing the World with Love

It is impossible to bless and judge at the same time. So hold constantly as a deep, hallowed, intoned thought the desire to bless, for truly then shall you become a peacemaker, and one day you shall behold, everywhere, the very face of God.

—PIERRE PRADERVAND

Discovering Blessing

Each night before bed, Beth and her daughter Sam complete their bedtime routine. After a story, a final drink of water, and a cozy tuck-in, Beth asks Sam, "Who would you like to send blessings to tonight?" Sam thinks a minute, then responds. There's her best friend from school, her grandparents who live far away, and her dog. "May they have blessings," Beth replies.

This is as close as Beth and her family come to prayer. They don't describe themselves as religious people, although I see deep spirituality in them—from the way they intentionally structure their lives for times of rest and work, to the simple "we are grateful for this food" they say before eating.

Always curious about the spiritual practices of others, I asked Beth about how the blessing practice worked for them. Beth described how she started it to ritualize generosity and thoughtfulness toward others.

"It's a way of putting good energy out into the world. And it feels peaceful to us, too," she added.

When I began researching the role that spiritual practices can play in raising hopeful, resilient children, this conversation came back to me. I was already implementing rituals of blessing with the children I work with, and I'd done a deep dive into Christian theology, trying to figure out how blessing "worked." (This is like any of the musings on how prayer works. It leads to as many questions as answers.) I realized that my short conversation with Beth all those years before, scribbled down in my notebook and tucked away, might hold the key: blessing ritualizes generosity, empowers and calms the blessing-giver in times of worry, and aligns us with the movement of Spirit, or as Beth said, it puts good energy out into the world.

Blessing is a way of allowing God to work more fully in us and through us. I chose to focus on "blessing" rather than more generally on "prayer" for this book in part because of this early conversation. I was particularly intrigued that Beth's practice of blessing appeared to transcend religious tradition.

Because my work often sits at the intersection of the secular and spiritual, and because I'm in conversation with people of other faith traditions, I'm always interested in the practices that connect people to the innermost part of themselves, no matter how they understand that. So, I offer this look at blessing as one particular prayer practice with the knowledge that it might open itself to you in different ways. Some may come to it specifically because it doesn't feel like prayer, and others may find in it an extension of a prayer practice they already have. Others of you, like me, may start out in a bit of uncertainty about this ritual and come to understand it differently through experience. I trust that the practice itself will become the teacher.

TRY THIS: *Add an element of blessing to a family routine. At a meal time, bedtime, or on the way to school, ask your family who they'd like to bless. For kids unfamiliar with the idea of blessing, you can say something like, "Who would you like to send God's light to today?" or "Who would you like to send love to today?"*

Blessing in Christian Tradition

When my daughter was about five years old, the church we attended held a blessing of the bikes service one Sunday morning. I dutifully wrestled our bikes onto the back of my silver Toyota Camry and drove them to the church. I had no idea what to expect, but "take your bike to church day" was, if nothing else, a way to connect our life at home with our church experience.

Wearing shorts and a t-shirt, the pastor used a water bottle to sprinkle water on each of the bikes, offering a prayer for protection and joy for the rider. To each handlebar, she tied a thin white ribbon to serve as a reminder that we had been blessed. That ribbon dangled off our bikes all summer, slowly becoming gray and tattered but always bringing a smile to our faces. Like the focus object people sometimes use in meditation, this ribbon seemed to pull me back to God's presence each time I saw it flapping in the wind.

When I recounted the experience to my atheist mother-in-law, she asked about the blessing. "Did it work?" she asked. "Like, did it prevent you from having accidents or something?" I'd wondered the same thing myself years before when taking part in a different "blessing of the bikes." That time, though, the bikes in question were motorcycles and I was the one giving the blessing.

Each year, the church I then served was the staging ground for a Poker Ride as a fundraiser for a civic group. Tradition held that the pastor of the church would bless the bikes before they took off on their ride through the Virginia backroads, winding back for a town festival. I gamely agreed but secretly wondered what exactly a blessing entailed. I knew we blessed food before eating, and said blessings over the waters of baptism and the bread and cup for communion. I knew, too, that the benediction I gave at the end of church services was a blessing. The difference was, I had years of church tradition to draw on for those blessings. I had never seen anyone bless a motorcycle, and I wasn't quite sure what such a blessing might mean.

In the end, I prayed for the riders to find joy, to be of service, and to ride safely and sent them on their way. No one complained that I had done it wrong, and I set aside my theological ponderings about what exactly *is* a blessing.

My experience with the second blessing of the bikes, and my mother-in-law's question, caused me to ponder again. The challenge is that often, blessing-giving is associated with magical thinking. Magical thinking is the idea that a person can make something happen by wishing it into existence, or by saying just the right words in just the right way. It's a common misconception we have about forms of prayer. Since I don't believe that God is a wish-granting machine, her question stumped me. Obviously, blessing a bike might not prevent bike accidents. (Although now that I think of it, we didn't have any accidents that summer.) Despite my inability to put words to the experience, I knew something meaningful had happened. I pondered this tension. What is the purpose of giving blessings, and how can it be a meaningful part of our lives?

Christian tradition offers muddled answers. There are so many accounts of biblical blessing-giving that it's difficult to come up with a clear definition of what's happening. Blessing spans a wide variety of ideas:

- A blessing makes something holy, or sets it aside for a special purpose, as in the blessing of the seventh day in Genesis 2:3 (NIV): "Then God blessed the seventh day and made it holy . . . ."

- A blessing is also something that people can become, as when Abraham is told, "I will make of you a great nation, and I will bless you, and make your name great, so that you will be a blessing" (Genesis 12:2). In this story, he is given a blessing so he can be a blessing. His existence blesses others.

- We also often talk about blessings in light of wealth, possessions, or health as in Proverbs 10:22 (NIV): "The blessing of the Lord brings wealth, without painful toil for it."

- Lastly, a blessing is something that people can give God. Psalm 103:1, for example, says, "Bless the LORD, O my soul, and all that is within me, bless his holy name." This broadens its meaning considerably. In this context, a blessing appears to be something like worship.

Some of these ideas are easier to wrap our heads around than others. The idea of "blessing" as material goods or physical health is perhaps one of the more challenging. There is always the danger that this material view creeps into prosperity gospel teachings, which is the idea that people are rich or healthy because of their faith—which isn't true to the wider biblical arc. It also leads to a belief that if you're poor, or sick, or struggling in some way, it's a sign of God's disfavor.

In Luke's account of the beatitudes, Jesus confronts this problematic theology head-on when he says, "Blessed are you who are poor, for yours is the kingdom of God." He lists three more surprising blessings: those who are hungry, those who weep, and those who are hated (Luke 6:20–22). It's clear from Jesus's teachings that blessings are not measured only in wealth, health, or even happiness.

Seeing our material possessions as a blessing can be an act of gratitude. I know many faithful people who say things like, "I've been blessed with a good job" or "I was blessed with good health," as a way of acknowledging the unearned gifts in their lives. There is a necessary creative tension between seeing the blessings we have without justifying those blessings as something we earned through our good faith or works.

Remembering the role that the Bible plays as a sacred conversation or a Beautiful Book, I lift all these examples of blessing as a way of saying, "Yep, it's complex." So if you haven't encountered the idea of blessing-giving before, or you've never really understood what it does, you're not alone. How does it work? When does it work? Is it mostly about us becoming better people, or does a blessing really change the world somehow?

This is a gift of contemplative practices We can recognize the mysteries as we live into our spirituality. It is similar to the experience of falling in love. We can't understand it until we've experienced it. We might yearn for it, we might talk about how it works from the angles of biology, psychology, and spirituality, but those explanations pale in comparison to the experience of loving and being loved.

Giving and receiving blessing is transformational—for each of us and for the world. I see blessing-giving as a way of aligning our desires with what Jesus called the kingdom of God. As John O'Donohue says, "A blessing is a circle of light drawn around a person to protect, heal, and strengthen." It's helpful to me to think of a blessing as an allowing, rather than a forcing. That is, God is already working in the world. Our response to that work is crucial. When we allow the Spirit of God to flow through us, we are making room for God's continued work. The "energy" we put into the world, as Beth described it, either lets God's love flow freely or it creates a stoppage in our souls. Like water, God's love will always find a way. Also like water, it flows strongest when it has a clear path.

TRY THIS: *Meditate on the idea of God's love flowing through you like water. Find a comfortable place to sit and imagine the flow of love from the top of your head to the bottom of your feet. Sit with that image for several minutes. What sensations do you notice in your body during and after the meditation? How does it feel in your mind and heart?*

Blessing with Children: Participating in God's Healing

Fall of 2019 brought with it news of devasting fires around the world. Many people rushed to help, as they so often do. Donations were taken to buy a section of the Amazonian rainforest in order to protect it from further deforestation. When fires consumed much of Australia, patterns for koala mittens and carrying pouches showed up online. Worried as we were, we wanted to be part of the healing.

One Sunday morning, I told the story of Jesus's baptism with a group of children. I suspected that they, too, had heard of fires raging around the world, and I was curious about the connections they might make between the spiritual significance of water and the news of the fires. We explored the story together, thinking about John the Baptist's role in preparing the way for Jesus. We talked about baptisms today. In my tradition, we don't often practice baptism by immersion, so a few kids wondered about the practice of getting baptized by "swimming in a river. What if we still did that?" they asked excitedly, then gasped in delight when I said that some people do get baptized that way. "Have you ever done that?" they asked, disappointed when the answer was no.

"What do you think it could mean to get baptized with a lot of water like that?" I asked them.

"It could be, like, how much love God had. Lots of water would make sure you knew there was lots of God's love."

All the kids agreed. "But sometimes when people don't have a lot of water, that still means God loves them," one added. "Yeah, sometimes we need to share water just like we share God's love," another added.

"Hmmm . . . ." I grabbed the bowl of water I'd planned to use at the end of children's worship. "If you could send water to someone as a symbol of God's love, who would you send it to?" One by one, the kids took a bit of water, held it in their palm, and named someone who needed a reminder of God's love, until one child said, "I'd send real water AND God's love to the Amazon!" "Oh, yeah," the others chimed in. "I'd send it like this!" the first child demonstrated, scooping up a handful of water and flinging it into the air. "I'd send lots and lots. Lots of love and lots of water."

"Let's bless the Amazon with water then," I said. "You can do it anyway you want." Some of the kids continued quietly holding a small bit of water in their hands, while others scooped up larger amounts, letting it drip out of their hands like rain. A few others mimed splashing water all over the place, the way you might in a splash fight at your local pool or lake.

It eventually got silly, as it would if you let a group of kids scoop handfuls of water and fling them around in church. But once we settled down again, several kids remarked on how good it felt to bless the world that way.

"My heart feels like it connected with God's heart," said one kid.

"It's nice to add our love to God's love. I hope all the water and all the love makes its way there."

What the kids experienced in that moment of "sending love and water" is the power of blessing as an avenue of healing. They practiced meeting the world's hurt with the healing power of love.

I was once in a yoga class for healing when the instructor invited us to bring peace into our spirits. "There's a lot going on in the world. We can't meet those needs with anxiety. We can't just worry and worry. People in need of healing don't need all of our anxiety rushing at them. They need our peace."

While I've certainly prayed the frantic, even frenetic, prayers of the desperate, this instruction changed the way I think about prayer and blessing. Sometimes when we feel our need or the needs of the world so deeply, we hold that need in prayer the way a pot bubbles over. Anxious thoughts roll over anxious thoughts as we plead for God's intervention.

What the practice of blessing offers us, as illustrated so well by the children, is a way of channeling those same desires into a practice that is—in itself—transformational. It shifts our internal energy, calming us and making us better able to cope with hardship. That alone is a gift to the world.

TRY THIS: *One blessing practice came to me from a fellow pastor I worked with at a safehouse for people leaving domestic violence.*

It works well for both kids and adults. Imagine you have small balls of light along your shoulders. Each ball of light is a blessing. As you think of a person or situation you'd like to bless, take a ball of light from your shoulder and send it to that person or situation. The light expands to form a bubble of love, protection, or healing around the person or situation.

The Great Longing: Blessing the Children

When God blesses the first people in the Genesis story of creation, God is making known their true identity as beloved children. In church life, we do this when we baptize a child or adult; we aren't turning them into children of God, we're acknowledging that they are already beloved of God and we are promising to help them live even more deeply into that.

At a time when global conversations center around topics as immense as overpopulation, human impact on the environment, and the myriad questions raised by technological development, people of all ages are asking questions that boil down to, "What value does my life hold?" I've heard kids ask it in ways like:

If the planet is overtaxed, will I be able to become a parent?

Why doesn't anybody understand the pressures we're feeling?

Why don't older generations like us? Why are we criticized so heavily for using technology that previous generations created?

Sometimes these questions come out in mock-playfulness, sometimes they come up in response to a Bible reading, sometimes they arise in one-on-one holy listening. While all of these questions are heavy-hitters, what's most troubling to me are the ones that hint at the generational divide. Every generation has a different culture, and to a certain extent, this leads to a gap in generational understanding. It looks like the generation gap may be widening.[1] Geographic mobility means kids are less likely to live near grandparents and other extended family members. Economic policies that pit the needs of old and young turn us into competitors rather than resource-sharers.

From studies of kids who've experienced trauma, we know that a child's ability to thrive despite difficulty is tied to the strength of their relationship with a caregiver. The more people a child has in their life who love them and affirm them, the more likely they are to face life's challenges with confidence. Kids need the love, support, and understanding from older generations. They need to know that they have value and that the world is better for their existence. The people who can give this are people who have experienced the world before each particular child was in it.

Once when Jesus was teaching and healing, some parents brought their children to him for blessing. In their overzealousness to protect Jesus's time and energy, his disciples stopped the parents. Jesus, however, insisted that the children be allowed to come for a blessing, saying that the realm of God belonged to them.[2]

The relationship of adults to children is a sacred one. When we bless a child, we meet them in their deepest longing: to be seen, known, and loved. A blessing, even one as simple as "you are a child of God," reassures kids that they are not a mistake. Further, it signals to them our confidence that they have the power to live into God's presence in this moment of re-creation.

In the early 1990s, Leanne Hadley opened First Steps Spirituality Center for children in Colorado Springs, Colorado. Her goal was to provide spiritual counseling for children recovering

1. William H. Frey, "Old Versus Young, the Cultural Generation Gap," Pew Trend Magazine, January 26, 2018, https://www.pewtrusts.org/en/trend/archive/winter-2018/old-versus-young-the-cultural-generation-gap.

2. Matthew 19:14, Mark 10:14, Luke 18:16.

from trauma. "There was no research on the topic yet, "Hadley said. "I just started creating space for children to come, and I'd listen and give them cookies and when they were done, I'd give them a blessing."[3]

Hadley's small nonprofit became the basis for her doctoral research and the development of what became known as "blessing-based spiritual nurture." She has gone on to become a leader in the field of children's spirituality. Her model has been adapted for use in church settings, hospitals, counseling, and homes.

Here's a general overview of how Hadley's "spiritual nurture" model works:

- Holy Listening—children share their experiences and feelings.

- Create a Sacred Space—if children are comfortable with prayer, they take time to build a sacred space, which lets them know that this is time with God.

- Prayer—children connect with God by coloring, playing with clay, sitting in silence, or some other developmentally appropriate prayer practice.

- Blessing—Hadley blesses the child, which she describes as "inviting God to work in the life of the child to bring healing." Her blessing is simple: she marks them with a blessing balm and says something like, "You are a blessing, go be a blessing."

It's the work of blessing the children that Hadley describes as being particularly significant. Hadley emphasizes that God is doing the work of healing, not her. Her role is simply to make space for the child to experience God's healing presence.

While I agree with this, I also see another way the blessing

---

3. Leanne Hadley, phone interview with the author, November 2018.

functions. When a person bares their soul, as they do in moments of deep connection, the blessing serves as a reminder that they are still loved. Their internal struggles or external circumstances can't change that. As kids continue to grow into adults wrestling with uncertainties, this gift of being loved will shape who they become and how they face those challenges.

TRY THIS: *Let your child know that they are a blessing. You can simply add "You're a blessing" to your "I love you" when you tuck them in at night. For older kids who tend to roll their eyes at these affections, try tucking a note in their lunchbox or putting a sticky note on the bathroom mirror. You could also say, "You're a gift to the world" or "I'm happy you came into our lives."*

Blessing: A Ritual for Parents

In a 2019 study of people receiving mental health care in California, a strong majority of people (seventy-three percent!) said that prayer was an important aspect of their mental well-being.[4] Time and time again I hear from people that it makes a difference in their lives. After using the balls of light blessing with a group of adults working on environmental justice, the whole room breathed more deeply. "Sometimes the urgency of this work makes me feel like I have to do it all by myself," said one person. "What a gift to remember that God is here with us." Another group, talking about the power of prayer, said that prayer helped them find hope in the eternal. "It's not like I pray and then I know that everything is going to be okay immediately. It's more like I pray and then I know that all of this belongs to God, and so do I."

---

4. A.-M. Yamada, D. Lukoff, C. S. F. Lim, and L. L. Mancuso, "Integrating Spirituality and Mental Health: Perspectives of Adults Receiving Public Mental Health Services in California," *Psychology of Religion and Spirituality* (2019), advance online publication, https://doi.org/10.1037/rel0000260.

Their comment is reminiscent of Julian of Norwich's well-known quote: "All shall be well and all shall be well and all manner of things shall be well." In prayer of all kinds, we enter this dance between wanting things to be different, even praying for God's healing to come, and also trusting that no matter what happens in our lifetime, the love of God continues. Acts of blessing give us a concrete way to invite God's healing into a situation while also letting go of our desire to control what happens. It's another paradox. We simultaneously step out in faith by believing in God's healing power while also going inward in faith to experience a sense of trust that transcends the need for certainty about the future.

Like the children who were given a way to express their fears about the world in our blessing of the Amazon, parents need a ritual of prayer and letting go. We know this instinctively. How often do we find our breath catching in our throats with the deep desire to ensure our children have good lives, while also knowing we have to entrust them to something bigger than our oh-so-human plans and hopes? Perhaps this is why many parents spontaneously create a ritual of blessing their children. One new mom described placing her hand on her baby's chest as she rocked the baby to sleep. "May God bless you and keep you," she said, drawing on the words from Numbers 6:24, which she'd heard many times during the church benediction.

In *Anxious Parents, Anxious Kids*, authors Reid Wilson and Lynn Lyons emphasize that the way adults cope with their worry directly impacts a child's ability to cope with worries of their own. As camp chaplain for a week-long church camp one summer, I saw this in action as experienced camp leaders handled homesickness with a no-nonsense, "You can handle this. It's going to be fun and you'll miss out if you go home." It wasn't easy for the kids to push through those homesick nights. "It'll pay off at the end of the week," several camp leaders reassured them. And they were right. All three of the kids who desperately wanted to go home mid-week arrived at Saturday smiling and cheerful. "I did it!" one kid said as they ran to their parents at pickup. "I missed you but I stayed and now I know I can come back next year!"

Parents, caregivers, and teachers are always balancing between keeping children from harm and empowering them to take risks and overcome failure. Every decision is monumental in this respect. (Do I let them watch scary movies? Take a mental health day from school? Ride their bike alone? Do they need more support from me? Less?) I haven't yet talked to a parent who is convinced they're getting this balance right all the time. Advice on how to achieve that is beyond what I can offer here, but I do know that it's a spiritual practice. It takes discernment and a willingness to mess up.

The practice of blessing our children and praying for their well-being is one way we can stay spiritually anchored in the midst of the urgent, uncertain work of parenting. When we're spiritually anchored, we're better able to parent out of our best, most trusting selves, for our own well-being, and for our children's.

TRY THIS: *Silently say a blessing for your child each night this week before you go to bed. Use the words of Numbers 6:24 or another prayer that expresses your desire to trust God is present in your child's life. See if it helps you feel calmer when making the hard parental decisions about when to let go and when to hang on.*

A Blessing for Seekers

Blessed are you who choose practices of faith, for you will know God's presence.

Blessed are you who open your heart to a child, for you will love deeply.

Blessed are you whose prayers bubble over, for you will know peace.

Blessed are you who seek calm in the storm, for you will know safe harbor.

Blessed are you, child of God, for you are beloved.

Questions for Group or Personal Reflection

1. What experiences have you had of being blessed or of blessing others?
2. What role does prayer have in your life? What role does it play in your family's life together?
3. If you've been baptized, or had your children baptized, what was that experience like for you?
4. How do you cope with the ever-present uncertainties and anxieties that come with having a child?
5. Who is someone in your life who encouraged you to take risks? How did they convey their trust in you?

Resources and References

Frey, William H. "Old Versus Young, the Cultural Generation Gap." *Pew Trend Magazine*, January 26, 2018. https://www.pewtrusts.org/en/trend/archive/winter-2018/old-versus-young-the-cultural-generation-gap.

Yamada, A.-M., Lukoff, D., Lim, C. S. F., & Mancuso, L. L. (2019). "Integrating Spirituality and Mental Health: Perspectives of Adults Receiving Public Mental Health Services in California." *Psychology of Religion and Spirituality*, Advance online publication. https://doi.org/10.1037/rel0000260.

Practicing Hope

What is hope? A group of elementary school students told me:

"Hope is like a voice that whispers to you, 'You can do this.'"

"Hope is when you think everything is bad but then you remember, God is still there."

"Hope is love plus courage."

"I have anxiety but sometimes when I'm really anxious, there's still a part of me that knows I won't always feel this way. That's hope."

I look at this list, and I see kids who will meet the challenges that come their way. They already trust God, and they know how to put their faith into action. The world is in good hands.

How we organize our lives says something about the God we believe in. When we choose to live in ways that embody hope and faith and courage, we can change the world.

So, what happens next?

There are no "one-two-three magic" steps in this book. Instead, you have some new insights on how spirituality connects to resilience and some ideas for spiritual practices to try. And what will happen is you'll try one or two, then the practice will slide a bit, and then maybe you'll try something else. That's part of being a practicing Christian, emphasis on *practicing*.

There is grace in recognizing this. I truly believe that any practices we do, even if we don't do them perfectly or as often as we mean to, make a difference. I liken it to musical training. What neuroscientists have discovered is that music changes our brain. When we listen to or play music, our brain activity increases. Our emotions can even shift, which we know from putting on cheerful music to lift a dull mood.

There are long-term benefits to playing an instrument. People who play instruments are healthier into old age. But here's the important part for us: people who play an instrument when they are children, even if they stop playing after a few years, still experience some protective benefits as adults. Yes, playing more and longer is better, but playing some still matters.

Little by little, one person and one family at a time, we can live as though the kingdom of God is among us. When we do, we'll discover that it truly is. Kids, with their ability to live in the present, their joy at the simple things, and their inherent awareness of God's presence, are our partners in this. The path may be challenging, but it is not impossible for us or for them.

I would love to hear how it goes for you. It means the world to an author to hear from readers. You can contact me online through ameliadress.com.

And now:

May the God who brought you here
bless your journey ahead.
In your sleeping and your serving,
your sharing and your receiving,
your mistakes and your repairing,
may you know God's presence.

Amelia Richardson Dress
Erie, Colorado
July 2020